SHIRLEY KING

DINING WITH MARCEL PROUST

A PRACTICAL GUIDE
TO FRENCH CUISINE OF
THE BELLE EPOQUE

FOREWORD BY JAMES BEARD

University of Nebraska Press
Lincoln and London

This book is dedicated to my daughter Amy and my mother.

Frontispiece: Proust (third from left) at table.
Detail of an illustration by Madeleine Lemaire
from Proust's *Les Plaisirs et les Jours*, 1896.

Library of Congress Cataloging-in-Publication Data
King, Shirley.
Dining with Marcel Proust: a practical guide to
French cuisine of the Belle Epoque / Shirley King;
foreword by James Beard.
p. cm.
Reprint. Originally published: London: Thames and Hudson, 1979.
Includes index.
ISBN-13: 978-0-8032-7826-4 (pbk.: alk. paper)
ISBN-10: 0-8032-7826-8 (pbk.: alk. paper)
1. Cookery, French—History—19th century.   2. Cookery,
French—History—20th century.   3. Proust, Marcel,
1871–1922—Knowledge—Manners and customs.   I. Title.
TX719.K56   2006
641.594409'034—dc22   2005028710

CONTENTS

FOREWORD

It is a pleasure to have a book come along that recaptures the glories of French bourgeois food in an earlier period – an unpretentious, savoury approach to cooking that has nearly been forgotten in the theatrics that now seem to surround French cuisine. Too often these days cookbooks are showpieces for the luminaries of the *Guide Michelin*. Witness the strenuous performances we have had by all the three-star chefs, who have deserted their stoves to tour the world, doing spectacular banquets for hundreds or highly publicized dinners for a dozen intimates. Their antics belong more to the stage than to gastronomy. Great food is not theatrical; it needs no fanfare; it does not have to be elaborate. What it requires is care, ingredients of the finest quality, and inspired taste, both in the preparation and in the presentation. Many a great dish can stand without a single garnish or even a sauce. The important thing is to produce food that gratifies the palate while it seduces the eye and the mind, an objective that becomes rarer and rarer in our kitchens. The Chinese, I think, are probably the only people who have not lost sight of this. Americans and Europeans are too frequently in pursuit of lavish gastronomic thrills.

Dining with Marcel Proust takes us back to traditions that sorely need revival. The connection between Proust and food is a natural one. He was a man who dealt in sensations, exquisitely examined, including those of the palate. In a celebrated passage, his remembrance of things past is set in motion by the recollection of the taste of a little cake, a madeleine, dipped in lime-flower tea. I feel that Proust must have had a deep sensual and intellectual appreciation of food. It is well known that he loved sitting at table with a circle of friends. I am certain he must have possessed the faculty I call 'taste memory'; that he enjoyed a good meal – whether a picnic, a luncheon in a garden or a formal dinner – not for the moment but for a lifetime, storing it in the memory, to be recalled at will.

This book evokes the spirit of Marcel Proust through the art of food. The brilliant essay by Shirley King provides the background for the Proustian table. The recipes are the true focal point. They present the basics of fine bourgeois cooking, simply and sensibly, reflecting an era of French cuisine at its most delicious. There is a genuineness and homely comfort about this food from the nineteenth and early twentieth centuries. It made imaginative use of the ingredients at hand and in season, and above all, it demanded the best that could be obtained. Of late, there are encouraging signs that we are finding our way back from theatrics to the sound virtues of bourgeois food. *Dining with Marcel Proust* will help get us there.

JAMES BEARD

INTRODUCTION

Within the first few pages of *A La Recherche du Temps Perdu* (Remembrance of Things Past), one becomes aware of the brilliantly told, minute observances of food which Proust weaves into his story. Very soon meals and culinary happenings become an integral part of the book. During the narrator's early life dinner time is all important – it is then that he dreads the approach of bed time, knowing that he must leave his mother's company for the night. Later, dipping a 'petite madeleine' in a cup of tea gives the narrator 'an exquisite pleasure' and evokes for him the memory of Combray, where his aunt lived. The cook was Françoise:

> No sooner had we arrived in my aunt's hall than we saw in the gloom, beneath the frills of a snowy cap as stiff and fragile as if it had been made of spun sugar, the concentric waves of a smile of anticipatory gratitude. . . . It was Françoise, motionless and erect, framed in the small doorway of the corridor like the statue of a saint in its niche.
>
> 1,69

Proust continues the description of a country cook and the meals she provided:

> Upon the permanent foundation of eggs, cutlets, potatoes, preserves, and biscuits, whose appearance on the table she no longer announced to us, Françoise would add – as the labour of fields and orchards, the harvest of the tides, the luck of the markets, the kindness of neighbours, and her own genius might provide; and so effectively that our bill of fare, like the quatre-foils that were carved on the porches of cathedrals in the thirteenth century, reflected to some extent the march of the seasons and the incidents of human life – a brill, because the fish-woman had guaranteed its freshness; a turkey, because she had seen a beauty in the market at Roussainville-le-Pin; cardoons with marrow because she had never done them for us in that way before; a roast leg of mutton, because the fresh air made one hungry and there would be plenty of time for it to 'settle down' in the seven hours before dinner; spinach, by way of a change; apricots, because they were still hard to get; gooseberries, because in another fortnight there would be none left; raspberries, which M. Swann had brought specially; cherries, the first to come from the cherry-tree, which had yielded none for the last two years; a cream cheese, of which in those days I was extremely fond; an almond cake, because she had ordered one the evening before; a fancy loaf because it was our turn to 'offer' the holy bread. And when all these had been eaten, a work composed expressly for ourselves, but dedicated more particularly to my father, who had a fondness for such things, a cream of chocolate, inspired in the mind, created by the hand of Françoise, would be laid before us, light and fleeting as an 'occasional piece' of music, into which she had poured the whole of her talent. Anyone who refused to partake of it,

Lunch in the open air (Proust is standing third from the left). Mante-Proust Collection.

saying: 'No, thank you, I have finished, I am not hungry,' would at once have been lowered to the level of the Philistines who, when an artist makes them a present of one of his works, examine its weight and material, whereas what is of value is the creator's intention and his signature. To have left even the tiniest morsel in the dish would have shewn as much discourtesy as to rise and leave a concert hall while the 'piece' was still being played, and under the composer's very eyes.

At length my mother would say to me: 'Now, don't stay here all day; you can go up to your room if you are too hot outside, but get a little fresh air first; don't start reading immediately after your food.' And I would go and sit down beside the pump and its trough . . . on the bench without a back, in the shade of a lilac-tree, in that little corner of the garden . . . from whose neglected soil rose, on two steps, an outcrop from the house itself and apparently a separate building, my aunt's back-kitchen. One could see its red-tiled floor gleaming like porphyry. It seemed not so much the cave of Françoise as a little temple of Venus. It would be overflowing with the offerings of the milkman, the fruiterer, the greengrocer, come sometimes from distant villages to dedicate here the first-fruits of their fields. And its roof was always surmounted by the cooing of a dove.

I, 94–95

Even her utensils have the same fascination for the writer:

At the hour when I usually went downstairs to find out what there was for dinner, its preparation would already have begun, and Françoise, a colonel with all the forces of nature for her subalterns, as in the fairy-tales where giants hire themselves out as scullions, would be stirring the coals, putting the potatoes to steam, and, at the right moment, finishing over the fire those culinary masterpieces which had been first got ready in some of the great array of vessels, triumphs of the potter's craft, which ranged from tubs and boilers and cauldrons and fish kettles down to jars for game, moulds for pastry, and tiny pannikins for cream, and included an entire collection of pots and pans of every shape and size. I would stop by the table, where the kitchen-maid had shelled them, to inspect the platoons of peas, drawn up in ranks and numbered, like little green marbles, ready for a game.

1,163

Proust based his character of Françoise on various housekeepers, servants and cooks he knew in his life. One of them was his Aunt Elizabeth's housekeeper and cook at Illiers, the Combray of the book. Her name was Ernestine Ballou, 'a mediaeval peasant who had survived to cook for us in the nineteenth century.' Félicie Fitau cooked for the Proust family in Paris, and Nicolas and Céline Cottin were their housekeeper and cook from 1907 to 1914. The housekeeper who looked after Proust the last eight years of his life was Céleste Albaret, who did not have to cook very much for him, because he could not be persuaded to eat in his last years. His diet consisted mainly of fillets of sole, chicken, fried potatoes, ice cream, cakes, some fruit and iced beer. When asked why he kept to this diet, he replied, 'You know when you have eaten a good meal, you feel heavy and then you haven't a free spirit. I need to have a free spirit.'

(CA)

In spite of this, his books contain many descriptions of heavy meals and luxurious dinner parties and feasts in hotel restaurants:

In the big dining-room which I crossed the first day before coming to the smaller room in which my friend was waiting for me, it was of some feast in the Gospels portrayed with a mediaeval simplicity and an exaggeration typically Flemish that one was reminded by the quantity of fish, pullets, grouse, woodcock, pigeons, brought in dressed and garnished and piping hot by breathless waiters who slid over the polished floor to gain speed and set them down on the huge carving table where they were at once cut up but where – for most of the people had nearly finished dinner when I arrived – they accumulated untouched. . . . chafing dishes . . . had been lighted here and there to keep the late comers' plates from growing cold (which did not, however, prevent the dessert, in the centre of the room, from being piled on the outstretched hands of a huge mannikin, sometimes supported on the wings of a duck, apparently crystal, but really of ice, carved afresh every day with a hot iron by a sculptor-cook, quite in the Flemish manner).

V, 127, 128

Proust saw beauty even in the remains left after everyone had eaten:

I would now gladly remain at the table while it was being cleared. . . . Since I had seen such things depicted in water-colours by Elstir, I sought to find again in reality, I cherished, as though for their poetic beauty, the broken gestures of the knives still lying across one another, the swollen convexity of a discarded napkin upon which the sun would patch a scrap of yellow velvet, the half-empty glass which thus showed to greater advantage the noble sweep of its curved sides, and, in the heart of its translucent crystal, clear as frozen daylight, a dreg of wine, dusky but sparkling with reflected lights, the displacement of solid objects, the transmutation of liquids by the effect of light and shade, the shifting colour of the plums which passed from green to blue and from blue to golden yellow in the half-plundered dish, the chairs, like a group of old ladies, that came twice daily to take their places round the white cloth spread on the table as on an altar at which were celebrated the rites of the palate, where in the hollows of oyster-shells a few drops of lustral water had gathered as in tiny holy water stoups of stone; I tried to find beauty there where I had never imagined before that it could exist, in the most ordinary things, in the profundities of 'still life'.

IV, 235

Much further on in the book, the narrator pretends he is not interested in food, but his lover is relaxed and becomes intrigued by the cries of Paris:

'Oh!' exclaimed Albertine, 'cabbages, carrots, oranges. All the things I want to eat. Do make Françoise go out and buy some. She shall cook us a dish of creamed carrots. Besides, it will be so nice to eat all these things together. It will be all the sounds that we hear, transformed into a good dinner. . . . Oh, please, ask Françoise to give us instead a ray with black butter. It is so good!' 'My dear child, of course I will, but don't wait; if you do, you'll be asking for all the things on the vegetable-barrows.' 'Very well, I'm off, but I never want anything again for our dinners except what we've heard cried in the street. It is such fun. And to think that we shall have to wait two whole months before we hear: "Haricots verts et tendres, haricots, v'là l'haricot vert." How true that is: tender haricots; you know I like them as soft as soft, dripping with vinegar sauce, you wouldn't think you were eating, they melt in the mouth like drops of dew. Oh dear, it's the same with the little hearts of cream cheese, such a long time to wait: "Bon fromage à la cré, à la cré, bon fromage." And the water-grapes from Fontainebleau: "J'ai du bon chasselas."'

IX, 166, 167

One of the best dishes he describes, the *Boeuf à la Mode* made by Françoise, is used as a metaphor for the whole process of writing a novel:

Moreover, since individualities (human or otherwise) would in this book be constructed out of numerous impressions which, derived from many girls, many churches, many sonatas, would serve to make a single sonata, a single church, and a single girl, should I not be making my book as Françoise made that *boeuf à la mode* so much savoured by M. de Norpois of which the jelly was enriched by many additional carefully selected bits of meat?

XII, 417

The recipe for Boeuf Mode is on page 58. As well as this, I have included recipes ranging from the simplest of fresh country food to the more elaborate dishes which might have been served in a Paris home or restaurant at the beginning of this century.

The recipes are prefaced by quotations from Proust's works or from writings about him: those few that are not, are included because they are essential in some respect to the other recipes and typical of the time evoked for us by Marcel Proust.

References are given by volume and page number in the 12-volume collected edition *Remembrance of Things Past*, translated by C. K. Scott Moncrieff (vol. 12 by Andreas Mayor 1970) and published in 1955–56 by Chatto & Windus, to whom my thanks are due for their permission to print the quoted passages. Quotations from Proust's *Jean Santeuil* are taken from the translation by Gerard Hopkins published by Weidenfeld & Nicolson in 1955; their permission is gratefully acknowledged. (Page references are to the paperback edition published by Panther books in 1966.) References given thus – CA, 98 – are to *Monsieur Proust* by Céleste Albaret, his housekeeper in his last years. All other sources are given in full.

ACKNOWLEDGMENTS

I would like to thank my many friends for their encouragement, assistance and support. Special thanks to Judith Bledsoe, Mme Geneviève Bounin, R. H. Carter (fishmonger, Kentish Town), Jane Conway-Gordon, Janet Drummond, Emma Fisher, David Levitt, Mrs Jarvis Mead, Shirley Mowbray, Dr Robert Shields, David Wiggins and Allana Wilson. Also thanks to my editor, Ursula Whyte.

Hors-d'Œuvre, Soups and Pâtés

Hors-d'œuvre

Hors-d'œuvre can be hot or cold. If cold they are usually foods such as raw or cooked vegetables prepared beforehand, smoked meats, tinned/canned fish, fresh prawns/shrimps, eggs, olives or even presentable left-overs such as cold meat, fish or vegetables, dressed with mayonnaise or vinaigrette.

In France a luncheon or dinner often begins with one of the above items. Hors-d'œuvre *variés*, as the name implies, are a selection of several items, which may be served together at the beginning of a meal or, nowadays, even as a light luncheon. Any of the following are suitable:

artichoke hearts
hard-boiled eggs mayonnaise
cooked white haricot beans
black olives
celeriac rémoulade
mussels, oil and lemon
fennel slices, oil and lemon juice
radishes, unsalted butter
cucumber cut into julienne strips
dressed crab
herring fillets (rollmops)
potato salad
cooked peeled prawns/baby shrimps
smoked hams, salamis
grated carrots
gherkins
tinned/canned hearts of palm with sour cream
green pepper slices, vinaigrette sauce
stuffed eggs
sardines
mushrooms
beetroot salad
red cabbage salad

Caviar

Caviar should always be served cold directly from the receptacle it is received in, or from a silver dish set on a bed of crushed ice. Accompaniments are not necessary, but quarters of lemon, blini and sour cream may enhance the event. Thin toast or Melba toast, finely chopped onion and finely chopped hard-boiled egg white and yolk can accompany caviar. The choice is yours.

Dining with Saint-Loup in the restaurant at Rivebelle, Marcel describes the 'incessant revolution of the countless servants. . . . No doubt they were running, one to fetch the hors d'oeuvre, *another to change the wine or with clean glasses.'*

IV, 153

French waiters and waitresses: an illustration from *Harper's Monthly Magazine*, 1889. Mansell Collection.

Blini

	UK	US	
30 g	1 oz.	1½ Tb	fresh yeast, *or*
15 g	½ oz.	1 Tb	dried yeast
115 ml	4 fl. oz.	½ cup	warm water
120 g	4 oz.	scant cup	white flour
120 g	4 oz.	scant cup	buckwheat flour
	½ tsp	½ tsp	salt
30 g	1 oz.	2 Tb	butter
300 ml	½ pint	1¼ cups	milk
	2	2	eggs, separated
30 g	1 oz.	2 Tb	butter, for frying

Makes 20–24 little Russian pancakes

At dinner at Mme Swann's, 'by the side of my plate I found a carnation, the stalk of which was wrapped in silver paper. . . . This custom, strange as it was to me, became more intelligible when I saw all the male guests take up the similar carnations that were lying by their plates and slip them into the buttonholes of their coats. . . . Another usage, equally strange to me but less ephemeral, disquieted me more. On the other side of my plate was a smaller plate, on which was heaped a blackish substance which I did not then know to be caviare. I was ignorant of what was to be done with it but firmly determined not to let it enter my mouth.'*

III, 173

Dissolve the yeast in the warm water for 15–20 minutes. Sift all the white flour and a quarter of the buckwheat flour together into a large bowl. Make a well in the flour, add the yeast mixture and stir with a large wooden fork or spoon, adding a little more warm water if necessary to get a sticky but smooth mixture. Cover with a cloth and place the bowl over a bowl of warm water or leave it to rise in a warm place such as the airing/linen cupboard or on top of a slow oven, for 1 hour.

When the mixture has risen, beat the egg yolks. Heat the milk gently with the butter, until the butter melts. Cool to lukewarm; then stir in the rest of the buckwheat flour, the salt and the egg yolks. Now gradually add the milk and butter to the dough, whisk well and let the batter stand for another hour.

After the hour, beat the egg whites until they are stiff and fold into the batter. Leave for 15 minutes.

Heat a small (about 4½-in.) frying pan over medium heat, add a little butter and pour in just enough of the batter to cover the bottom of the pan. A larger pan can be used, as the batter does not spread easily. Turn the blini over when the edges begin to brown and cook the other side. Proceed with the rest of the batter, adding more butter to the pan as needed. Serve as soon as they are made, or keep them warm in a very low oven, gas mark 1, 275°F. Delicious with sour cream and caviar.

These pancakes freeze well, but should be reheated briefly in a hot oven before serving.

Melba Toast

Thinly sliced brown or white bread.

Toast the slices lightly, cut off the crusts and carefully divide each piece into two, using a sharp knife. Toast again or dry out in an oven (gas mark 4, 350°F) for 10 minutes.

A characteristic of this toast is that it curls and bends, so don't worry if it does just that, during the second toasting.

Oysters · Huîtres

Oysters have been a prized dish throughout the centuries. Greeks and Romans enjoyed these molluscs, as many do nowadays, serving them as hors-d'œuvre. Several types are found in different waters. In England the 'Helford' and 'Whitstable' have flat, roundish shells and are held in high esteem. The 'Portuguese' have the long, deeper and more craggy shells.

In France the famous *belons* are the favourites. They are the *plates* (flat, roundish shells) from Brittany, but they are becoming scarce. The *creuses* and *spéciales* from Brittany, which are graded by size, are delicious. In the south-west of France the *plates* are called *marennes* and *gravettes*. The *creuses*, called *claires*, *fines de claires* and *spéciales de claires*, seem to melt in the mouth.

The East Coast of the USA produces Blue Points (Long Island), Chincoteagues (Chesapeake Bay) and Cotuits (Cape Cod). Olympias come from the West Coast.

Oysters are best eaten raw. They must be fresh, and alive when opened. They survive well for 3–4 days while they get rid of their impurities, but certainly not longer than 8 days.

Serve on the hollow half shell, which retains their liquor, on top of a bed of crushed ice. Accompany with lemon quarters and a plate of buttered rye or brown bread.

Petite Marmite

Beef, veal, marrow bones, chicken giblets, vegetables and water are simmered together very slowly in a large pot. The broth is served from the dish with French bread. It may also be clarified for use as consommé.

	UK	US	
about 2 kg	4½ lb.	4½ lb.	back rib of beef tied, or topside (rump roast or boneless chuck)
about 1 kg	2 lb. 3 oz.	2 lb. 3 oz.	veal knuckle or neck of veal
	2	2	beef marrow bones
500 g	1 lb.	1 lb.	chicken giblets (hearts, necks, gizzards, livers)
	4	4	medium onions
	6	6	carrots
	1	1	small turnip
	2	2	sticks celery
	3	3	sprigs parsley
	1	1	sprig thyme
	3	3	leeks
	½	½	small cabbage (optional)
	1½ Tb	1½ Tb	salt
	2	2	egg whites and their shells for clarifying (optional)

Place the meat, bones and chicken giblets in a very large *marmite* (stockpot) or saucepan. Fill with cold water to nearly cover the contents and bring to the boil over medium heat.

Prepare the vegetables; leave the skin on the onions if they are brown, for it will add colour to the soup. Scrape the carrots and cut into 2-inch lengths. Peel the turnip and cut into quarters. Wash and strip the celery and tie in a bundle with the parsley sprigs and thyme. Trim the leeks and wash well. Quarter the cabbage.

The soup will take about half an hour to start simmering; at this point be ready to take off any scum that rises to the top. A nylon tea-strainer with very fine mesh is the best tool for this job. Otherwise, a slotted spoon will serve.

When the soup is clear, put in the vegetables (except for the leeks), herbs and seasoning, and cover loosely with a lid to allow some of the steam to escape. The heat under the soup should be very low, so that the liquid just barely shudders. If it cooks too quickly the meat will shrink and toughen; besides, the soup will lose its clarity as the fat emulsifies with the water.

Cook for 4 hours, putting in the leeks and cabbage (if used) in the last hour and the chicken livers in the last 20 minutes so that they will not overcook.

This soup is traditionally served direct from the stockpot.

If making consommé, strain off the rest of the soup and refrigerate overnight. Next day, carefully skim off all the congealed fat, then heat the soup to boiling and reduce for 20 minutes by continued boiling over medium heat. To clarify the broth, beat two egg whites to a froth and add to the soup with the egg shells. Reduce heat and simmer for 10 minutes. Strain through a sieve lined with cheesecloth.

*"'I can't explain it to you very well,"
he told me once. "I think you take
specially chosen pieces of beef, with
chicken gizzards and various other
little things. And it must simmer for a
long time, over a low fire. But it is
delicious."'*

CA, 98

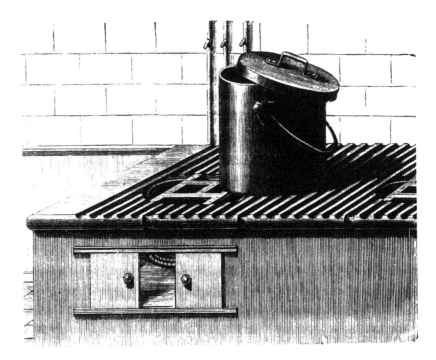

Pot au feu, from *La Cuisine
d'aujourd'hui* by Urbain Dubois,
1900.

Watercress Soup · Soupe au Cresson

	UK	US	
	3	3	bunches of watercress
350 g	12 oz.	2 cups	peeled and cubed potatoes
250 g	9 oz.	1½ cups	chopped onions
100 g	3 oz.	¾ cup	chopped leeks
	1	1	clove of garlic (optional)
30 g	1 oz.	2 Tb	butter
	1 Tb	1 Tb	oil
1 litre	1¾ pints	4½ cups	water
	2 tsp	2 tsp	salt
			pinch of allspice
150 ml	¼ pint	⅔ cup	single/light cream

Serves 6

'No sooner was the order to serve dinner given than with a vast gyratory whirr, multiple and simultaneous, the double doors of the dining-room swung apart; a Chamberlain bowed before the Princesse de Parme and announced the tidings "Madame is served", in a tone such as he would have employed to say "Madame is dead", ... the couples moved forward one behind another to the dining-room, separating when they had reached their places where footmen thrust their chairs in behind them; ... other doors opened through which there entered the steaming soup.'

VI, 173–4

Wash the watercress. Cut off the stalks and chop them. Melt the butter with the oil in a large, heavy saucepan. Add the potatoes, onions, leeks, the watercress stalks and the garlic. Sauté the vegetables over medium heat for 10 minutes, stirring occasionally. Add the water, the salt and the allspice. Bring to the boil and simmer for 10–15 minutes, until the potatoes are soft. Add all but a few leaves of the watercress to the hot soup and put through the medium mesh of the mouli food mill. A lot of stalks and roughage cannot be pushed through the mill, so discard them. The soup will have tiny specks of the bright green watercress for colour. Liquidize the soup in batches; this helps to prevent it from separating, if it is not served right away. Add the cream and heat again. Sprinkle each bowl of soup with the remaining watercress leaves.

This soup can equally well be served cold, in which case chill thoroughly before serving.

Tables laid for the Fête des Acacias, given by the Comtesse de Castellane in July 1896. Georges Sirot Collection.

Leek and Potato Soup ·
Potage Bonne Femme

	UK	US	
450 g	1 lb.	4 cups	trimmed, washed and chopped leeks
230 g	$\frac{1}{2}$ lb.	$1\frac{1}{3}$ cups	chopped onions
700 g	$1\frac{1}{2}$ lb.	4 cups	peeled and cubed potatoes
30 g	1 oz.	2 Tb	butter
	1 Tb	1 Tb	oil
1 litre	$1\frac{3}{4}$ pints	$4\frac{1}{2}$ cups	water
	1 Tb	1 Tb	salt
			ground white pepper
			pinch of grated nutmeg

Serves 6–8

Melt the butter with the oil in a heavy saucepan and add the chopped leeks, onions and potatoes. Let the vegetables sweat over medium heat with the lid on for 10 minutes, stirring from time to time.

Add the water, salt and pepper and bring to the boil. Simmer for 10 to 15 minutes until the potatoes are just tender. Remove from the heat and add the nutmeg. Serve immediately.

'Terrifying as I always found these meals, in the vast restaurant, generally full, of the mammoth hotel, they became even more terrifying when there arrived for a few days the Proprietor (or he may have been only the General Manager, appointed by a board of directors) not only of this "palace" but of seven or eight more besides, situated at all the four corners of France, in each of which, travelling continuously, he would spend a week now and again. Then, just after dinner had begun, there appeared every evening in the doorway of the dining-room this small man with white hair and a red nose, astonishingly neat and impassive, who was known, it appeared, as well in London as at Monte Carlo, as one of the leading hotel-keepers in Europe. . . . I felt that even the movements of my spoon did not escape him, and were he to vanish after the soup, for the whole of dinner the review that he held would have taken away my appetite.'

III, 377–8

A fashionable restaurant in Monte Carlo, 1907. *Illustrated London News.*

Pâté

The ingredients of a pâté or terrine can include a variety of minced/ground meats, fat and livers, but with the addition of chicken breasts and slices of tongue and pistachio nuts it becomes more than a simple luncheon dish, and can be served as a first course for dinner.

	UK	US	
230 g	½ lb.	½ lb.	veal
230 g	½ lb.	½ lb.	lean pork
230 g	½ lb.	½ lb.	pork fat
125 g	¼ lb.	¼ lb.	ham or tongue
230 g	½ lb.	½ lb.	chicken livers
	1	1	chicken breast
	6	6	slices fat pork (blanched) or bacon (streaky)
55 ml	2 fl. oz.	4 Tb	cognac
	2	2	eggs
225 ml	8 fl. oz.	1 cup	dry white wine
			grated rind of ½ lemon
	1	1	clove of garlic, chopped
	10	10	juniper berries, crushed
	½ tsp	½ tsp	thyme
	¼ tsp	¼ tsp	mace
	¾ tsp	¾ tsp	salt
			freshly ground black pepper
	20	20	pistachio nuts, shelled (optional)
			gherkins to garnish

Serves 12

Have the butcher mince/grind the veal, pork and pork fat together, or mince/grind the meats and fat on the large-hole plate of the mincer/grinder. Put the meats in a bowl with the thyme, juniper berries, mace, garlic and wine and marinate for 2 hours. At the same time marinate the chicken livers in the cognac. After marinating, put the chicken livers and the eggs in the blender and liquidize for 10 seconds. Mix very thoroughly with the minced meats, pistachio nuts, lemon rind, salt and pepper.

Cut the chicken breast in eight long strips. Cut the ham or tongue into strips ½ inch wide.

Set the oven to gas mark 2, 300° F. Flatten and stretch the strips of bacon with the back of a knife and lay three of them in the bottom of a terrine or pan about 12 in. long by 4½ in. wide, or of about 2 litres/3½ pints/9 cups capacity. Put one-third of the meat mixture on the bacon and lay 4 chicken breast strips in 2 lines down the terrine, two by two, with strips of ham or tongue on top. Then add another third of the mixture, the remaining strips of breast and ham or tongue and the final third of the mixture. Lay the remaining three strips of bacon on the top and cover with aluminium foil. Put the terrine in a baking tin with hot water to a depth of approximately 1 in., and cook for 1½ hours. Remove the aluminium foil and cook for a further ¼ hour.

Let it cool, without unmoulding, for 2 hours and then weight the pâté, to facilitate cutting later on. Find a dish or pan of a similar size to put on top of the pâté and place some objects (such as jam jars) weighing about 2 kg/4 lb. on it. Leave for several hours or preferably overnight in the refrigerator for the flavour to mature. Unmould, and garnish with gherkins.

Hare Pâté · Terrine de Lièvre

	UK	US	
	1	1	hare, dressed
700 g	1½ lb.	1½ lb.	belly of pork/fat pork
300 ml	½ pint	1¼ cups	red wine
	12	12	juniper berries, crushed
	3	3	cloves of garlic, crushed
	½ tsp	½ tsp	dried thyme, or sprig of fresh thyme
			salt
			pepper
			gherkins to garnish
			some chicken stock may be needed to thin down the pâté

Serves 12–14

In the kitchen at 'Tante Léonie's' house in Illiers-Combray there stands a long brown terrine, its lid in the form of a hare. All terrines and pâtés were served from this to the Proust family.

Cut the pork into small pieces, removing any bones. Remove the sinews and fine membranes from the hare and cut into pieces. Place the pork and pieces of hare in a bowl, pour in the wine and leave to marinate overnight.

Next day, set the oven to gas mark 1, 275 °F. Put the pork, hare, wine, juniper berries, garlic, thyme, salt and pepper in a heavy casserole. Cover and cook for 4 hours. Leave to cool.

Pick off all the hare and pork meat from the bones and fat. Discard the pieces of fat and the bones, but reserve the stock, which may have jelled as it cooled. Put the meat in a bowl and, with a fork in each hand, pull it apart into shreds (this is similar to the method of preparing rillettes).

Reheat the stock, strain it over the meat and stir well. Taste for seasoning and stir in additional warm chicken stock if necessary, to give the mixture a spreadable consistency.

Blend the pâté in batches in the liquidizer to a slightly smoother consistency. Pour into a terrine or a lightly buttered mould. Refrigerate for 2 hours.

Bring the pâté to room temperature before serving, to bring out its flavour and help it to spread well on hot bread or toast. If using a mould, loosen the sides with a knife, invert on to a serving dish and decorate with fanned sliced gherkins.

Galantine of Turkey · Galantine de Dinde

'To make a galantine well, you must make a business of it, and it is much the best way to go to M. Dumas of 55, Prince's Street, Leicester Square, and buy it. The terrines which are sold in the shops under the name of Yorkshire pies are not Yorkshire pies but galantines in pots. Buy them if you have near you – worthy namesake and rival of the great Alexander – a Dumas who can make a romance out of the breast of a turkey, and a scene out of the merry-thought of a chicken, raise a pheasant into a personage, put wit into a pistachio, and endue a truffle with the soul of poetry.' (From *Kettner's Book of the Table* by E. S. Dallas, 1877.)

It is hardly likely that the reader will have Dumas near him today to make this fabulous galantine, but the following recipe can perhaps help to make a Dumas out of him.

Preparation of the galantine, although a fairly simple procedure, should be started 3 days before serving, so as to ensure time for the flavour to mature. The galantine will keep well in the refrigerator for 3–4 days longer.

'"There you go," said Mme Verdurin, "you frighten him, you make fun of everything he says, and then you expect him to answer. Come along, tell us . . . and you shall have some galantine to take home," said Mme Verdurin, making a cruel allusion to the penury into which Saniette had plunged himself by trying to rescue the family of a friend.'

VIII, 113

	UK	US	
2·3–2·8 kg	5–6 lb.	5–6 lb.	turkey, dressed
	1	1	pheasant
			half a medium-sized chicken
120 g	¼ lb.	¼ lb.	pork belly
	1	1	piece of pork fat (to bard the galantine during cooking)
	2 Tb	2 Tb	cognac
	about 50	about 50	shelled pistachio nuts
	1	1	black truffle
175 g	6 oz.	⅔ cup	chicken fat
115 ml	4 fl. oz.	½ cup	red wine
	12	12	juniper berries, crushed
	2	2	pinches of *quatre épices*
	1½ tsp	1½ tsp	salt
	½ tsp	½ tsp	freshly ground black pepper
	½ tsp	½ tsp	freshly ground nutmeg
			pinch of mace
	1 Tb	1 Tb	chopped parsley
			gherkins, tarragon leaves, red pepper, chives etc. for decoration

Serves 12

To bone the turkey, cut the skin along the back with a small, sharp knife. Gradually cut the flesh away from the carcase, bearing in mind that the leg and wing bones remain attached to the carcase and that therefore the meat must simply be carved away from these bones. Discard, or reserve for another use, the second and third wing joints and cut away the tendons from the leg flesh. Always be careful to keep the skin whole, except of course where the legs and wings are placed. Reserve the thigh bones. When all the bones have been removed, spread the turkey, skin side down, on a board or platter.

Cut the flesh from the pheasant and chicken, keeping the breasts and other large pieces whole; marinate the pheasant flesh in 2 tablespoons of cognac overnight. Cover the turkey with greaseproof paper and leave overnight.

Next day, prepare the pistachio nuts; pour boiling water over them, let them steep for 5 minutes, then drain them and slip off their skins. Set the oven to gas mark 4, 350° F. Roast the nuts for 10 minutes.

Leaving a $\frac{1}{2}$-in. layer of flesh attached to the turkey skin, pare off much of the flesh, keeping the larger pieces and a good deal of the breasts whole. Pull the wing skins to the inside, and if the leg skins are still complete (no holes or splits, except where the joints were cut), they too can be stuffed. Stuffing the legs is optional and depends on whether you want the finished galantine to look like a turkey. Make sure that the skin is covered with flesh, placing extra flesh where it is thin. Sprinkle with salt and pepper and flatten with a wooden mallet.

Now sort out the larger pieces of pheasant, turkey and chicken flesh, putting the small pieces apart to be minced/ground in the liquidizer. There should be about 900 g/2 lb. of flesh to mince/grind. Add some of the larger pieces to make up this amount if necessary. Mince/grind in the liquidizer in small batches, then mix in a large bowl with the chicken fat, wine, juniper berries, *quatre épices*, salt, pepper, nutmeg, mace and parsley. Using a mincer/grinder if desired, mince/grind all together twice, using the medium plate of the mincer/grinder.

Cut the larger pieces and pork belly into long thin strips. Cut the truffle into small cubes or rounds.

Spread a third of the forcemeat over the turkey breasts. Cover the whole surface with long lines of half the strips of pork belly, pheasant, chicken and turkey, sprinkle over the pistachio nuts, and place pieces of truffle down the middle. Spread another third of the forcemeat on, then strips and nuts again and a final layer of forcemeat.

Strengthen the rigidity of the legs by sticking the thigh bones in with the leg filling.

Have a needle and buttonhole thread or thin string ready. Pull together the two sides of the back and sew neatly, repairing any small holes there may be in the skin. The galantine will now resemble a soft cushion. In order to improve its shape, place it in a long, narrow pan that will fit it snugly (approximately 10 × 6 in.), wedging small saucers or something similar along the sides if necessary to push it into shape.

Set the oven to gas mark 4, 350° F. Place a piece of pork fat over the top of the galantine and bake for 2 hours, basting occasionally and pouring off the liquid that has appeared after 1 hour. Reserve this stock. Remove the pork fat in the last 15 minutes so as to brown the skin lightly. Remove the galantine from the oven, pour off all liquid and let it cool overnight.

Next day, carefully take off the fat that has congealed on the surface of the now jellied stock, and gently reheat the stock. Pour through cheesecloth into a shallow pan and refrigerate again to obtain a clear jellied aspic. Also refrigerate the galantine at this time.

Before serving, wipe off the grease, if any, from the galantine, remove the stitching and place on a serving dish. Heat 2 tablespoons of the aspic gently, let it cool a little, but use it before it sets again. If it is a hot day, it may be necessary to add gelatin to the aspic to make sure it stays set. In this case, stir a teaspoon of gelatin into 1 tablespoon of water, heat over simmering water until dissolved and mix with the aspic. Cool the aspic again.

Brush a layer of aspic on the cold galantine, then decorate with tarragon leaves, slivers of red pepper, strips of leeks for flower stalks, spinach or lettuce leaves cut into small, delicate leaves, rounds of tomato peel for flower centres, chives and spring onions/scallions for stalks etc. Dip these in aspic before placing on the galantine. Brush more aspic all over. The aspic must be liquid and the galantine cold for this operation to succeed. Refrigerate the galantine again.

Remove the galantine from the refrigerator 2 hours before serving, so that it can be savoured at room temperature. Chop the rest of the aspic into little cubes or diamonds and serve round the edge of the galantine, with fanned sliced gherkins.

Rillettes

Rillettes are made in many districts of France, but those made in Tours and Le Mans are the most famous. Pork and herbs are cooked very slowly and finely shredded, then potted and sealed with a layer of fat for long preservation. Rillettes are usually served as a pâté with salad or as an hors-d'œuvre with French bread. The mixture spreads easily and can be used for sandwiches.

	UK	US	
450 g	1 lb.	1 lb.	lean pork
450 g	1 lb.	1 lb.	pork fat
	6	6	juniper berries, crushed
	3	3	cloves of garlic, crushed
	½ tsp	½ tsp	thyme
	1½ tsp	1½ tsp	salt
			freshly ground black pepper
115 ml	4 fl. oz.	½ cup	water
	3	3	sprigs of parsley, tied with thread

Serves 4

Set the oven for gas mark 1, 275° F.

Cut the meat and fat into very small cubes. Put into a heavy casserole with the juniper berries, garlic, thyme, salt, pepper, water and parsley. Cover and cook for 5–6 hours until the cubes of fat have all but melted and the meat begins to brown. Stir occasionally.

Drain the meat in a sieve, reserving the fat, and let it cool. Remove the parsley. Put the meat in a bowl and pound it with a mortar or wooden spoon, then pull it apart using a fork in each hand. The texture should be shreds rather than a smooth paste.

Taste for seasoning, making sure the meat is salted enough. Pot the rillettes in a small terrine or earthenware pot. Take 4 tablespoons of the fat, melt it and strain it over the rillettes. They will keep well in the refrigerator for several weeks.

Foie Gras

Foie gras is one of the great delicacies of gastronomy. It is produced in Alsace and south-west France and is the liver of specially fattened geese and ducks, available from November each year. Delicious tins or pots of truffled foie gras pâtés and whole foies gras can be bought, at considerable cost. Foies gras are not readily available to us, whereas the livers of ordinary geese and ducks are much easier to obtain and, although much smaller, have good qualities. Since these livers freeze well, it is possible to collect goose or duck livers as they become available, freezing them until there are enough for the following recipe (2 goose livers or 4 duck livers). Chicken livers are almost universally available by weight, fresh or frozen.

At a dinner party given by the Verdurins: 'an extraordinary procession of plates . . . and what is perhaps equally rare is the really altogether remarkable quality of the things served upon these plates, food delicately manipulated, a stew such as the Parisians, one can shout that aloud, never have at their grandest dinners. . . . Even the foie gras bears no resemblance to the insipid mousse which is generally served under that name . . .'

XII, 19–20

An arrangement for pâté de foie gras, from *La Cuisine d'aujourd'hui* by Urbain Dubois, 1900.

Goose, duck or chicken liver in pastry · Foie Gras en Croûte

This dish makes an aromatic and delicious first course.

	UK	US	
230 g	½ lb.	½ lb.	goose, duck or chicken livers
	1	1	truffle (optional)
	2 Tb	2 Tb	cognac or Armagnac
			salt, pepper
	5	5	thin slices fat pork (blanched) or bacon (streaky)
	1 tsp	1 tsp	thyme (fresh or dried)
	1 Tb	1 Tb	goose, duck or chicken fat or butter
175 g	6 oz.	6 oz.	puff pastry (see recipe, p. 156)
	1	1	egg yolk

Serves 8

Gently remove any threads or fibres from the livers, sprinkle with salt and pepper and soak in the cognac for 2 hours at room temperature. Stud with fine slices of truffle if desired. Line a small terrine with the slices of fat pork or bacon and set the oven to gas mark 4, 350° F. Put the livers on top of the bacon, spread with the fat and sprinkle with half the thyme. Cover with more bacon and the rest of the thyme, and put the lid on. Cook for 30 minutes, take out of the oven and leave to cool.

Forty-five minutes before serving, roll out the pastry to a large square (about 14 inches square), reserving some pastry for decoration, and place the livers and bacon in the middle. Moisten the edges of the pastry with water, then pull up opposite corners and fold together. Repeat the process with the remaining two corners, so that the package has the appearance of an envelope. Decorate with the extra pastry. Set the oven to gas mark 6, 400° F. Mix the egg yolk with a teaspoon of water and brush over the pastry. Make two holes in the pastry to let the steam escape. Bake for 25 minutes or until the pastry looks crisp and golden.

Chicken Liver Mousse ·
Mousse de Foie de Volaille

The following recipe can hardly be classed, by anyone's standards, as an 'insipid mousse'.

	UK	US	
230 g	½ lb.	½ lb.	chicken livers
	1 tsp	1 tsp	cognac
			salt, pepper
	3	3	eggs
90 g	3 oz.	¾ stick	butter
115 ml	4 fl. oz.	½ cup	double/heavy cream
			capers for decoration
45 g	1½ oz.	3 Tb	butter, to seal the top of each mousse

for white sauce:

	UK	US	
45 g	1½ oz.	3 Tb	butter
45 g	1½ oz.	⅓ cup	flour
300 ml	½ pint	1¼ cups	milk

Serves 8

Remove the fibrous strings from the livers and marinate with the cognac, salt and pepper.

Make a white sauce by melting the butter over medium heat. Stir in the flour and let it cook for a minute. Add some of the milk and stir briskly until the sauce is thick, then add the remaining milk and whisk if necessary to make sure of achieving a smooth sauce. Leave to cool.

Melt the butter. Put the chicken livers, eggs and melted butter in the blender and liquidize for 15 seconds.

When the sauce has become lukewarm, add the chicken liver mixture and some additional salt, and stir well. Strain through a sieve to remove any lumps. Beat the cream until stiff and fold into this mixture.

Set oven to gas mark 4, 350° F.

Butter 8 little individual ramekins and fill with the mixture. Set them in a roasting pan with ¾ in. hot water and bake for 35 minutes.

Leave to cool completely.

To seal and decorate the tops of each mousse, melt the butter and pour on a thin layer. Place three capers on top of each mousse. This mousse will keep 2 days in the refrigerator.

Serve with hot toast.

Baked Eggs with Cream ·
Œufs en Cocotte à la Crème

These eggs are cooked in little ramekins until the whites have set, but the yolks must remain soft. A choice of different purées can be placed under the egg to enhance the dish. Although it is possible to bake these little dishes in the oven, one has more control if they are cooked on top of the stove.

		UK	US	
		4	4	eggs
15 g		½ oz.	1 Tb	butter
60 ml		2 fl. oz.	4 Tb	double/heavy cream
		4 Tb	4 Tb	spinach or watercress purée (optional)
		4 tsp	4 tsp	grated Parmesan cheese to sprinkle on top (optional)
				salt, pepper

Serves 4

'On days when I was going anywhere with the Swanns I would arrive in time for déjeuner, which Mme Swann called "le lunch"; . . . if, at this hour when ordinarily I did not perceive them, I seemed now to be discovering the fine weather, the cold, the wintry sunlight, it was all as a sort of preface to the creamed eggs . . .'

III, 139

Butter 4 individual ramekins. Set them in a frying pan with ½ in. of hot water over a low heat and bring the water to simmering point.

If using a purée, put 1 tablespoonful in the bottom of each ramekin and heat thoroughly, for about 5 minutes, before adding the egg. Break the eggs individually into a cup to make sure the yolk remains whole. Put aside any yolks that do break. Carefully pour each egg into a ramekin, sprinkle with salt and pepper (and cheese if desired) and cover with a lid or aluminium foil. Cook for 8–10 minutes, uncovering from time to time to discover exactly when the whites of the eggs have set. (This will take slightly longer when a purée is used.) When you see this beginning to happen, heat the cream in a saucepan and be ready to pour it on top of the eggs, as you call your guests to the table right away.

Luncheon Dishes

Bouchées à la Reine

These were named after Marie Leszczynska, wife of Louis XV, who was very fond of the large vol-au-vent served in those days to several guests at a time. Her chef created the smaller individual 'bouchées' that are known nowadays as 'vols-au-vent'.

For a luncheon or dinner dish, individual bouchées are filled with chicken, mushrooms and sweetbreads. Buy 8 vol-au-vent cases, ready-made or frozen, or make your own using the recipe below. Smaller bouchées are served as hot hors-d'œuvre.

		UK		US	
750 g		1 lb. 10 oz.		1 lb. 10 oz.	puff pastry (see recipe, p. 156) or two 375 g/13 oz. packets of frozen puff pastry
		1		1	egg
		1 tsp		1 tsp	milk

for the filling:

		UK		US	
		2		2	chicken breasts
					water to cover
350 g		¾ lb.		¾ lb.	mushrooms
120 g		4 oz.		1 stick	butter
90 g		3 oz.		⅔ cup	flour
440 ml		¾ pint		2 cups	milk
		3 Tb		3 Tb	madeira
		2 tsp		2 tsp	lemon juice
					salt, pepper
120 g		4 oz.		4 oz.	prepared sweetbreads (optional, see recipe, p. 62)
		1		1	truffle cut into julienne strips (optional)
					parsley to garnish

Serves 8

Stages in the making of a *bouchée à la reine*, with special cutters for making the base. From *La Cuisine d'aujourd'hui* by Urbain Dubois, 1900.

Defrost the pastry, if frozen, for 1½ hours at room temperature.

Set the oven to gas mark 8, 450° F. Roll out the pastry to no less than ¼-in. thickness. The thickness is important, to achieve a well-risen bouchée case. With a pastry cutter 3½ in. in diameter, cut 16 circles. Moisten the top edges of 8 of them with water. Cut a smaller centre circle, 2½ in. in diameter, into but not quite through the other 8 and put one of these on to each of the first 8. With a knife, make small vertical incisions around the outside of the pastry case, a light criss-cross on the bottom, and a few cross marks on the top.

The trimmings can be used for fleurons (pastry crescents, see recipe, p. 157). It is useless trying to make more cases with the trimmings, because the pastry cannot rise well after being rolled a second time.

Brush only the tops of the bouchée cases with beaten egg and milk. Be careful to avoid brushing the inside or outside edges of the cases, as this will prevent the pastry from rising.

Place the bouchée cases on a baking sheet previously brushed with water. Cook 4 or 5 at a time, so that they are not overcrowded and the heat can circulate evenly. Bake for 25 minutes and when cool enough to handle, carefully lift off the 'lid' with the tip of a sharp knife and scoop out and discard the partially cooked pastry underneath.

For the stuffing, set the oven to gas mark 4, 350° F. Lay the chicken breasts in an oven dish with 300 ml/½ pint/1¼ cups of water. Cover with a lid and bake for 30 minutes.

Dice the sweetbreads and reserve them.

Wash and slice the mushrooms, and chop the stems. Fry them in 30 g/1 oz./2 Tb butter for 2–3 minutes over medium heat until they lose some of their moisture. Sprinkle 1 teaspoon of lemon juice over them and put them aside.

Drain the chicken, reserving its liquid; remove the bones and skin and discard them. Cut the chicken into small pieces.

Measure the stock and add milk to make it up to 700 g/1¼ pint/3 cups of liquid.

Melt 90 g/3 oz./¾ stick butter in a saucepan and add the flour. Stir well, until it is well amalgamated, then add the stock and milk. Stir constantly over medium heat until thick and smooth; add 2 tablespoons of madeira, 1 teaspoon of lemon juice, salt and pepper and just barely cook over very low heat for 10 minutes, stirring occasionally. Add the mushrooms and pieces of chicken, also the prepared sweetbreads, the truffle if desired, and 1 tablespoon of madeira, and heat through.

In the meantime, heat the bouchée cases in an oven at gas mark 4, 350° F., for 5 minutes. Pour the filling into them, cover with the pastry lids, garnish with parsley and serve.

At dinner at the Guermantes' the Duke is telling a story: '"The cooking at Zénaide's is not bad, but you would think it more ordinary if she was less parsimonious. . . . Zénaide insisted that Oriane should go to luncheon there . . . 'You must come,' Zénaide insisted, boasting of all the good things there would be to eat. 'You are going to have a purée of chestnuts, I need say no more than that, and there will be seven little bouchées à la reine.' 'Seven little bouchées!' cried Oriane. 'That means that we shall be at least eight!'"'

VI, 248

Dinner at the Guermantes': drawing by Philippe Jullien. From *Remembrance of Things Past*, published by Chatto and Windus Ltd.

Risotto with Squid · Risotto aux Calmars

	UK	US	
	I	I	clove garlic, chopped
	I	I	small onion, chopped
	4 Tb	4 Tb	olive oil
285 g	10 oz.	1¼ cup	round Italian rice (Arborio or Vialone)
115 ml	4 fl. oz.	½ cup	dry white wine
400 g	14 oz.	14 oz.	squid
			salt
			freshly ground black pepper

Serves 4

Clean the squid, removing the insides and head, but retain the tentacles. Remove the outer membrane and wash thoroughly. Cut the body into thin rounds and simmer in water together with the tentacles and 1 teaspoon of salt for 10 minutes.

In a heavy saucepan or casserole heat the oil and sauté the chopped garlic and onion over low heat until tender, but before they start to brown. Add the rice to the onions and stir occasionally for 3 minutes until the rice is permeated with the oil. Pour in the wine and let it bubble a little. Add the squid, its stock and a cup of hot water to the casserole. Cover with a lid and cook over a very low heat, adding more hot water, a cupful at a time, as it is absorbed, for 30–40 minutes, when the rice should be moist and tender. Season to taste with salt and freshly ground black pepper.

The Marquise de Villeparisis and her old lover, M. de Norpois, in a Venetian hotel: '"Here is the bill of fare. First of all, there are red mullets. Shall we try them?" "For me, yes, but you are not allowed them. Ask for a risotto instead. But they don't know how to cook it." "That doesn't matter. Waiter, some mullets for Madame and a risotto for me."'

XI, 297

Croque-Monsieur

	UK	US	
	8	8	slices of bread
	4	4	slices of ham
	4 or 8	4 or 8	slices of Swiss cheese – Gruyère or Emmenthal
			butter
			Dijon mustard (optional)
60 g	2 oz.	4 Tb	clarified butter (see recipe, p. 102)

Serves 4

Cut the crusts off the bread, and butter each slice. Make a sandwich filled with the ham, covered lightly with mustard, then the cheese and another slice of bread. Press firmly together. Melt half the clarified butter in a frying pan, over medium heat, and gently fry the sandwich until crisp on both sides. Serve immediately. Alternatively, make the sandwich filling with layers of cheese, ham, mustard, and cheese. If you possess a sandwich toaster, butter the outside of the sandwich before toasting. Clarified butter is not likely to burn because the sediment has been drained off.

'Well, as we came out of the concert, and, on our way back to the hotel, had stopped for a moment on the front, my grandmother and I, for a few words with Mme de Villeparisis who told us that she had ordered some croque-monsieurs *and a dish of creamed eggs for us at the hotel . . .'*

III, 389

Bacon Omelette · Omelette au Lard

2 large eggs
salt
pepper
butter
1½ slices of fat pork (blanched) or unsmoked bacon

This recipe is for an omelette for one person. If you wish to serve more, multiply the ingredients and use a large frying or omelette pan.

Fry the fat pork or bacon until it crisps, cut it into very small pieces and reserve it.

Break the eggs into a small bowl and add a sprinkling of salt and pepper; beat with a fork briefly until the eggs are blended.

Heat a 7-in. heavy frying pan or omelette pan over medium heat and melt a little butter in it. Before the butter browns, add the eggs and cook for 1 minute until they begin to set. Then tip the pan away from you and, using a spatula, lift a third of the omelette towards you, letting the liquid eggs run underneath. Cook for another minute or two and, when the eggs are almost set, sprinkle in the bacon bits and fold the omelette into three.

Wait a minute until it puffs up slightly, then roll on to a warm plate.

Other flavourings for omelettes can be:

Mushrooms, tomatoes, onions or shallots sautéed in butter
Fines herbes (chopped tarragon, parsley, chives and chervil)
Cooked asparagus tips or peas
Chopped parsley, lettuce or chicory/endive
Spinach purée
Cooked and chopped kidneys or chicken livers
Previously cooked mussels, oysters, prawns/shrimps, crab, salmon, salt cod/morue, crayfish tails, scallops
Smoked salmon, smoked haddock, smoked mackerel
Tuna fish
Lumpfish caviar, red or black
Grated Parmesan or Gruyère cheese
Sliced or julienned truffle
Shredded or cubed ham

'The sliding and sizzling of butter on the stove could have excited no more delicious quiver of appetite in his empty stomach than did the fretting of rain upon the roof, to which he lent an attentive ear only for an instant, the better to conjure up a picture of the lovely omelette, studded with bacon, which very soon now he would see being carried into the dining-room.'

Jean Santeuil, 506

Five-minute eggs · Œufs Mollets

Bring a saucepan of water to the boil, lower in the eggs with care and boil for exactly 5 minutes. Remove the eggs with a slotted spoon and rinse briefly under cold water. Tap each egg all over, on a plate or the table top, to break the shell. Peel off the shell carefully, for the yolk should still be soft and the white of the egg might break. (These eggs can be kept hot in warm water for a little while if the sauce is not yet ready.) Place the eggs on a serving dish and coat with the sauce, or alternatively heat the slices of ham in a frying pan and arrange them on a serving dish with the egg on the top, coated with sauce. A delicious light lunch.

Scrambled Eggs · Œufs Brouillés

3 eggs per person
1 small nut/tsp butter per person
salt, pepper
2 slices fat pork (blanched) or unsmoked bacon per person (optional)

Fry the bacon, put it in an oven dish and keep warm in a low oven, gas mark $\frac{1}{2}$, 250° F.

Break the eggs into a bowl, season with salt and pepper and add the butter in small pieces, reserving some of it. Whisk together well with an egg whisk. Melt the remaining butter in a saucepan and place on top of another saucepan of simmering water or in a *bain marie*. Add the eggs and stir constantly with a wooden spoon, until they solidify but are still soft and creamy. Pour over the dish of bacon and serve immediately.

Eggs with Cream Sauce · Œufs Béchamel

There are at least three dishes known as *Œufs à la Crème*. One is *Œufs en Cocotte à la Crème* (see recipe, p. 28); another is for boiled eggs (*œufs mollets*) served with a cream-and-Béchamel sauce, also called *Œufs Béchamel* (see recipe below); and another very similar method is to serve *œufs mollets* (or fried or poached eggs) with hot cream poured round them.

8 eggs (2 per person) or
4 eggs (1 per person) and
4 slices of ham

Serves 4

It is advisable to prepare the sauce before cooking the eggs.

	UK	US	
300 ml	$\frac{1}{2}$ pint	1$\frac{1}{4}$ cups	milk
	1	1	small onion
	1	1	small bayleaf
			sprig of thyme (optional)
			pinch of grated nutmeg
30 g	1 oz.	2 Tb	butter
30 g	1 oz.	4 Tb	flour
	1 tsp	1 tsp	salt
			white pepper
125 ml	4 fl. oz.	$\frac{1}{2}$ cup	single/light cream

Makes 430 ml/$\frac{3}{4}$ pint/2 cups of sauce

Heat the milk with the onion (cut in half), the bayleaf, thyme and nutmeg to just below boiling point. Melt the butter in a saucepan and then stir in the flour, off the heat, until well mixed. Strain in the flavoured milk and stir thoroughly until thick and smooth. Add the salt and pepper and barely cook over very low heat for 10 minutes, stirring occasionally with a whisk. This will ensure that the flavour of the sauce matures and the floury taste disappears. Stir in the cream before serving.

The sauce may be prepared beforehand and reheated in a bowl over simmering water. If it becomes lumpy, because a skin has formed on the top, rub through a sieve at the last moment.

Ravioli

Proust reported to his friend Paul Morand in March 1917, that every evening he received a dinner of ravioli, sent to him from outside by a person unknown to him, although it is thought his friend Antoine Bibesco did it for a tease, since Proust recalled telling him [Bibesco] how easy it was for him to dine at home 'just by sending out for some ravioli'.

  Paul Morand, Journal d'un Attaché
d'Ambassade

These ravioli can be served with butter and cheese or baked with tomato sauce. Both recipes are included here.

	UK	US	
450 g	1 lb.	3½ cups	flour
	4	4	large eggs

for the filling:

	UK	US	
230 g	½ lb.	½ lb.	veal
	5	5	slices of salami
230 g	8 oz.	1 cup	spinach
	2 Tb	2 Tb	freshly grated Parmesan cheese
	1	1	egg yolk
			salt, pepper
			nutmeg

if serving with butter and cheese:

	UK	US	
170 g	6 oz.	1½ sticks	butter
	8 Tb	8 Tb	freshly grated Parmesan cheese (or more)

tomato sauce:

	UK	US	
	2	2	medium-sized onions
	2	2	cloves of garlic
	1 Tb	1 Tb	oil
15 g	½ oz.	1 Tb	butter
	½ tsp	½ tsp	oregano
900 g	2 lb.	2 lb.	tomatoes, chopped, or 1 large can (794 g/1 lb. 12 oz.)
	2 tsp	2 tsp	sugar
			salt, pepper, nutmeg
115 ml	4 fl. oz.	½ cup	red wine (optional)
			grated Parmesan cheese

Serves 8

Sift the flour into a bowl and make a well in it. Beat the eggs with a fork and pour into the well. Stir thoroughly with the fork, gradually incorporating the flour. Pour this rough dough on to a table top or board and knead vigorously for 10 minutes without extra flour until it is a smooth, pliable dough. Let it rest 1 hour.

For the filling, mince/grind the veal and salami together, using the small-hole plate. Fry lightly in a little oil. Cook the spinach, drain it, chop it finely and add it to the meat with the grated Parmesan and the egg yolk. Flavour with salt, pepper and nutmeg.

Divide the paste in two and roll out very thinly on a floured board or table top, making two sheets each approximately 14 by 20 inches. Measure off and lightly mark 1½-inch squares and put little coffee-spoon measures of filling in the centre of each square. With a pastry brush and some water, wet the edges of the squares. Wet the other pastry sheet and, wet side down, place it on top of the squared-off paste. Press down with the fingers in between the fillings, in lines, both ways so that the pastes stick together well. Let it rest for 30 minutes before finally cutting the squares with a pastry cutter or a sharp knife.

Bring a saucepan of water to the boil, add 2 teaspoons salt to the water and drop 10 ravioli in at a time. Cook for between 8 and 15 minutes, depending on the dryness of the ravioli. Remove with a slotted spoon to drain on a teacloth. Serve with melted butter and grated Parmesan or with tomato sauce.

Tomato sauce

Chop the onions and the garlic and fry in the oil and butter until golden brown. Add the oregano, tomatoes, sugar, salt and pepper. Simmer for 1 hour and then push through the medium mesh of the food mill twice.

When the ravioli are cooked, cover the bottom of an oven dish with a thin layer of tomato sauce, then a layer of ravioli, more sauce, and Parmesan. Continue to layer in this fashion, finally topping with small pieces of butter. Cover and heat for 10–15 minutes in the oven at gas mark 5, 375° F. Uncover for the last 5 minutes.

Stages in the making of ravioli, and (*right*) toothed cutting wheel. From *La Cuisine d'aujourd'hui* by Urbain Dubois, 1900.

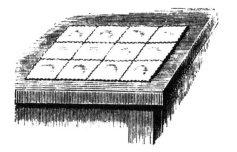

Fish and Seafood

Bouillabaisse

The true bouillabaisse originates on the Mediterranean coast of France and is a fish soup or stew consisting of a variety of Mediterranean fish and shellfish, which must include the *rascasse* (known only on the Mediterranean) to make it authentic. You can choose as few or as many varieties of fish as you want to. It is cooked for a short time with fish stock and wine, onions, tomatoes, leeks, garlic, various herbs and spices including saffron, and is served with slices of French bread, sometimes toasted, sometimes fried in butter.

Other forms of bouillabaisse are made with fish from the Atlantic. Another fish stew, called a *matelote*, is made with freshwater fish. A fish soup made on the Normandy coast is prepared with cider (instead of white wine); Calvados and cream are added before serving.

Before preparing a bouillabaisse it is advisable to visit a fishmonger (or two) to choose 6 types of fish, such as: (1) some firm white fish or some fillets of sole/flounder, (2) some eel and (3) squid, (4) small red mullet/red snappers if available, and (5 and 6) two shellfish, such as mussels and prawns/shrimps or clams.

It is a wonderful dish to serve for a dinner, because most of the preparations are easy and can be accomplished beforehand, it requires a very short cooking time, and it results in a thoroughly satisfying and flavoursome dish.

To make a bouillabaisse for 8 people, choose approximately 2·3 kg/5 lb. of different fish and shellfish from the following selection (US substitutes or equivalents in brackets): fillets of whiting (weakfish), sole (flounder), plaice, lemon sole or John Dory; firm white fish such as turbot, brill, halibut, anglerfish, conger or rock eel, haddock, cod, sea bass (striped bass); small red mullets and gurnets (red snappers); shellfish such as oysters, prawns (shrimps), scampi, lobster, crabs, scallops, mussels and clams.

	UK	US	
225 ml	8 fl. oz.	1 cup	olive oil
60 g	2 oz.	½ stick	butter
	2	2	medium onions
	4	4	small leeks
	4	4	medium tomatoes
	3	3	cloves of garlic, crushed
	3 Tb	3 Tb	fresh fennel bulb, chopped
115 ml	4 fl. oz.	½ cup	dry white wine
			salt, pepper
			cayenne
			large pinch of saffron (0·5 g)
	2	2	large slivers orange peel
	1	1	large sliver lemon peel
	5	5	sprigs of parsley chopped
			French bread

'''*Come along, my good Brichot, get your things off quickly. We have a* bouillabaisse *which mustn't be kept waiting.*'''

VIII, 63

for the fish stock:

115 ml	4 fl. oz.	½ cup	dry white wine pinch of thyme bay leaf water

N.B. The liquid from mussels or clams and the flavour of squid are specially good for the soup.

Prepare a fish stock with the fish bones, wine, thyme, bayleaf and enough water to cover. Bring to the boil and simmer, covered, for 45 minutes.

Prepare the French bread by either frying slices in butter, or rubbing with garlic and toasting, or have it ready to serve plain.

Fillet the fish if necessary, or if the fishmonger has not done it. To clean the squid, remove the insides, cut the tentacles from the head and reserve, and cut the body into rounds. Scrape the mussels with a sharp knife, remove encrustations and beard, scrub with a wire or nylon scourer and rinse in several changes of fresh water. Scrub the clams.

Cook the mussels and clams in a covered saucepan over medium heat for 5–10 minutes until the shells open. Reserve the shellfish and their liquid, discarding any that do not open. Boil the lobster and crabs in salt water for 20 minutes; leave to cool, cut the lobster into pieces and reserve. Cut the firm white fish into 2-inch cubes. Cut the eel into 1-inch slices.

Pour boiling water over the tomatoes, let them steep for 1 minute, drain and peel them. Chop roughly, discarding the seeds. Finely chop the onions. Wash and trim the leeks, removing most of the green part; chop roughly.

Heat the oil and butter in a large casserole or saucepan and fry the onions over medium heat, without browning them, for 10 minutes.

Add the leeks and garlic and cook for 3 minutes. Add the tomatoes, chopped fennel, orange and lemon peel, wine, fish stock (strained through a sieve) and the mussel or clam liquid (strained through cheesecloth because it may be sandy). Add salt, pepper, 2 pinches of cayenne and the saffron.

(The above preparations may be done beforehand and the final cooking can be left until just 25 minutes before serving time: 10 minutes to bring the soup to simmering point, and 15 minutes to cook the fish.)

Bring the soup to the boil and add the fish, putting in those pieces that need longer cooking first, such as the firm white fish, eel, squid and red mullet/red snappers. Boil hard for 2 minutes to amalgamate the oil and water, then add the rest of the fish and the shellfish: fillets, lobster, mussels, prawns/shrimps, clams. Total cooking time is 10–15 minutes and no longer, because the fish tends to break up if overcooked.

To serve pour the soup into a bowl and arrange the fish carefully and decoratively on another dish, unless your casserole is suitable for bringing to the table. Sprinkle the fish with chopped parsley and serve with slices of French bread.

Lobster à l'Américaine ·
Homard à l'Américaine

One theory regarding the name of this dish is that it should correctly be 'à l'Armoricaine', i.e. as cooked in Brittany (Armorique being the old name for Brittany). However, the sauce is not at all Breton, but typically Provençal, with tomatoes and garlic essential to it, and many people prefer the theory that it was invented by a restaurateur named Pierre Fraisse, born in Sète, who went to Chicago, returned to Paris, opened a restaurant called Peter's, served turtle soup and roast beef, and named his lobster dish after the Americans who were among his clients.

The delicious flavour that the fresh lobster shell gives to this dish is essential, and for this reason it is necessary to buy the lobster alive and kill it just before cooking. This operation can be performed by the fishmonger (if he is willing), but it must then be rushed home and cooked immediately.

Of course, if you are willing to forgo the distinctive flavour of freshly cooked shell, then kill the lobster by plunging it into boiling water.

'A dish of hot lobster, set in readiness for Mademoiselle de Réveillon who never ate eggs, added to the pleasing smell of zinnias and snapdragon a fragrance which was not, as was theirs, an end in itself.'

Jean Santeuil, 270

	UK	US	
	1	1	lobster, weighing approximately 1.1 kg/2½ lb.
90 g	3 oz.	6 Tb	clarified butter
	1½ Tb	1½ Tb	oil
	4	4	small shallots or spring onions/ scallions, chopped
	2	2	leeks (white part only), chopped
	½	½	carrot, coarsely grated
	1	1	clove of garlic, crushed
	4	4	sprigs parsley
	1 Tb	1 Tb	tarragon
	6	6	medium tomatoes skinned and roughly chopped
	1 Tb	1 Tb	tomato paste
	1 Tb	1 Tb	cognac
150 ml	¼ pint	⅔ cup	dry white wine
			salt, pepper
			pinch of cayenne

Serves 2

If desired, wear oven gloves or rubber gloves to handle the lobster. Place it on a board, and with a sharp knife kill it by cutting the tail away from the body. Wait a few minutes until the muscles of the lobster stop moving. Try to reserve any liquid that comes from the lobster. Turn it upside-down and split the body and tail lengthwise. Cut off the claws and crack them. Remove the sac from the head, and put aside the coral, if any. Cut the tail into 2 or 3 smaller pieces, and put all the pieces in a bowl. Season with salt and pepper.

Heat the butter and oil in a frying pan and add the lobster pieces. Cook over medium heat for 10–15 minutes, turning occasionally, until the shells are bright red. Lower the heat, sprinkle over the cognac and set alight. When the flames have died down, transfer the lobster to a casserole and keep warm over low heat.

Brown the shallots, leeks, parsley carrot and garlic in the same frying pan, adding more butter and oil if necessary. Stir in the tomatoes, tarragon, tomato paste, white wine, salt, pepper, cayenne and any liquid from the lobster. Simmer for 10 minutes and rub through the medium mesh of the mouli food mill (optional) on to the lobster. Simmer for another 15 minutes, adding the coral in the last 2 minutes.

Table centrepiece featuring a lobster, from *La Cuisine artistique* by Urbain Dubois.

Grilled/Broiled Red Mullet with Fennel · Rougets au Fenouil

Céleste Albaret (Proust's housekeeper in his last years) mentions in her book M. Proust *that Proust liked to eat red mullet. They had to be small; from Marseilles; and she had to buy them from Maison Prunier, near the Madeleine, because nowhere else were they so fresh or so succulent and the right size. He remembered his father used to buy them from Prunier's.*

1 red mullet per person, weighing approximately 230 g/½ lb. each, or 2 small mullet per person
olive oil
salt
pepper
fresh fennel bulb (60 g/2 oz./½ cup per person)
lemon or orange (¼ per person)

Scale and clean the mullet, removing the gills and entrails but, if desired, leaving the liver, which is considered a delicacy. Score the fish and sprinkle inside and out with oil, salt and pepper.

Grill/broil the mullet under medium heat for 5 minutes on each side, turning once. In the meantime, cut the fennel into julienne strips and toss in hot oil in a frying pan for 2–3 minutes. Peel the lemon or orange, removing all the pith, and cut into sections, adding any juice that drips to the fennel as it cooks. Add the fruit sections and warm through. Pour this garnish over the grilled/broiled fish.

Brill · Barbue

The velouté sauce or the quick cream sauce can be prepared while the brill is baking, but the optional cream sauce benefits from long cooking, and preparations should be started beforehand.

	UK	US	
	1	1	brill weighing approximately 1 kg/2 lb. 3 oz., cleaned, and head off (in USA, one could use a piece of halibut)
115 ml	4 fl. oz.	½ cup	dry white wine
	1 tsp	1 tsp	salt
	4	4	fleurons (puff pastry crescents, see recipe, p. 157)
			velouté sauce (see recipe, p. 99), *or*
			cream sauce (see recipe, p. 100), *or*
			quick cream sauce, see below

optional garnish:

	UK	US	
	12	12	mussels, steamed as recipe, p. 43
	4	4	scallops cooked with the brill in the last 10 minutes

Serves 4

Place the brill in an oven dish and cover with the wine and the same amount of water. Sprinkle it with salt and leave to marinate for 1 hour at room temperature.

Set the oven to gas mark 5, 375° F. Bake the brill for 40 minutes. Drain off the liquid. Arrange the brill in a serving dish and pour the sauce over it. Serve with plain boiled rice (see recipe, p. 158) and garnish with fleurons. Also garnish with mussels and scallops if desired.

To prepare brill with quick cream sauce:

	UK	US	
100 ml	4 fl. oz.	½ cup	double/heavy cream salt, pepper

Set the oven to gas mark 5, 375° F. Bake the brill for 35 minutes. Drain the liquid from the brill into a saucepan, replace the brill in the oven on a lower shelf and re-set to gas mark 2, 300° F. Boil the liquid over medium heat for about 15 minutes, until reduced to approximately 170 ml/6 fl. oz./¾ cup. Add the cream, salt and pepper and boil again over medium heat for a few minutes until the sauce has reduced further and thickened. Serve the brill with the sauce poured over, as above.

'It is a delight for the imagination and for the eye, I do not fear to say it, for the imagination of what used to be called the gullet, to have served to one a brill which has nothing in common with that kind of stale brill served on the most luxurious tables which has received on its back the imprint of its bones during the delay of the journey, a brill not accompanied by that sticky glue generally called sauce blanche *by so many of the chefs in great houses, but by a veritable* sauce blanche *made out of butter at five francs the pound; to see this brill in a wonderful Tching Hon dish graced by the purple rays of a setting sun on a sea which an amusing band of lobsters is navigating, their rough tentacles so realistically pictured that they seem to have been modelled upon the living carapace, a dish of which the handle is a little Chinaman catching with his line a fish which makes the silvery azure of his stomach an enchantment of mother o' pearl.'*

XII, 20

Mussels · Moules Marinière

	UK	US	
2·3 litres	2 quarts	2·3 quarts	mussels (approximately 40)
45 g	1½ oz.	3 Tb	butter
	2	2	shallots (or 1 small onion)
	4	4	sprigs of parsley
	2	2	small carrots (optional)
	1	1	leek
	2	2	cloves garlic, crushed (optional)
	½ tsp	½ tsp	fresh or dried thyme
100 ml	4 fl. oz.	½ cup	dry white wine

Serves 4

Rinse the mussels in several waters, cut off the beards, scrape them clean of any barnacles or encrustations with a sharp knife, and then scrub with a wire or plastic scourer. Discard any that are open or do not close when tapped. Cover with a wet cloth and keep in a cool place until ready to cook.

Finely chop the shallots or onions, parsley, carrots and leek. Melt the butter in a saucepan, add the vegetables and cook over medium heat for 7 minutes until the shallots and carrots begin to brown. Add the garlic, thyme and mussels and stir. Pour in the wine and cover with a lid. Cook for 10–15 minutes, shaking the pan occasionally and checking to see when all the mussels are open. (Discard any that do not open.) Serve immediately in soup bowls with all the liquid.

From the cries of Paris: '"A la moule fraîche et bonne, à la moule!" "Ah! Mussels," said Albertine, "I should so like some mussels." "My darling! They were all very well at Balbec, here they're not worth eating."'

IX, 165

Front of the Grand Hôtel, Cabourg, on which Proust based the hotel at Balbec. Bibliothèque Nationale.

Pike Quenelles · Quenelles de Brochet

Method of shaping quenelles.
From *La Cuisine d'aujourd'hui* by
Urbain Dubois, 1900.

Serve with prawn sauce (recipe, p. 100) or the sauce for which the recipe is given below. Pampille (Mme Léon Daudet), in her book *Les bons plats de France*, gives a recipe for quenelles which calls for equal proportions of fish, *panade** and butter. The following recipe does not require so much butter.

		UK	US	
700 g		1½ lb.	1½ lb.	pike (or whiting), *or*
350 g		12 oz.	12 oz.	boned and skinned fillets of pike (or whiting)
panade:				
175 g		6 oz.	2 cups	fresh white breadcrumbs
150 ml		¼ pint	⅔ cup	milk
		1 Tb	1 Tb	rice flour
		2 tsp	2 tsp	salt
				pepper
		4	4	egg yolks
175 g		6 oz.	1½ sticks	butter
		2	2	egg whites
				dry white wine and water (to poach the quenelles in)
for the sauce:				
30 g		1 oz.	2 Tb	butter
30 g		1 oz.	4 Tb	flour
150 ml		¼ pint	⅔ cup	milk
150 ml		¼ pint	⅔ cup	dry white wine
		1 tsp	1 tsp	anchovy essence
		1 tsp	1 tsp	tomato paste
		1 tsp	1 tsp	lemon juice
				salt, pepper, cayenne

Serves 8

> '*Mme de Guermantes, whose vocabulary . . . was as savoury as those dishes which it is possible to come across in the delicious books of Pampille, but which have in real life become so rare, dishes where the jellies, the butter, the gravy, the quenelles are all genuine, permit of no alloy, where even the salt is brought specially from the salt marshes of Brittany.*'
>
> VI, 266

Pick over the flesh of the fish, remove any small bones or skin, and chop coarsely. Put in the blender in 3 batches and liquidize, stopping the machine frequently to stir and shift the flesh, making sure that it is all pulverized.

Make breadcrumbs by cutting the crusts off white bread and putting small pieces into the blender to produce fine crumbs.

Soak the breadcrumbs in the milk in a large bowl; stir in the rice flour and then the fish, salt and pepper. Using the electric beater, beat this mixture well, adding the egg yolks one at a time. Soften the butter by cutting it into small pieces on to a plate and heating briefly over hot water, or in a low oven. There is no need to melt the butter. Now add it, piece by piece, to the fish forcemeat, and beat until it is well blended. You may have to scrape the beaters clean every now and again. Whip the egg whites until stiff and fold into the forcemeat. Refrigerate for 1 hour so that the mixture can harden somewhat, and during this time prepare the sauce.

* A mixture of breadcrumbs, flour, eggs etc., to bind the fish mixture.

For this, melt the butter in a saucepan, add the flour off the heat and blend well, then add the milk and wine and stir over low heat until the sauce is smooth. Stir in the anchovy essence, tomato paste, lemon juice, salt, pepper and cayenne pepper. Simmer over very low heat for 20 minutes, stirring occasionally.

Form the forcemeat into cylinders 3 inches long and 1 inch thick, or into shapes of your choice. Fill a large frying pan two-thirds full with equal parts of water and dry white wine and bring to a faint simmer. Poach the quenelles for 10 minutes, turning carefully once. Lift out with a wire spatula or slotted spoon, place them in a warmed oven dish and pour the sauce over them.

They may be garnished with fleurons (pastry crescents, see recipe, p. 157).

Marcel and his friend Albertine listen to the street cries of Paris. "'J'ai de la raie toute en vie, toute en vie'' . . . "Oh please, ask Françoise to give us instead a ray with black butter. It is so good!'' "My dear child, of course I will, but don't wait; if you do, you'll be asking for all the things on the vegetable-barrow.''

IX, 165, 167

'Fish-market': painted tiles from a Paris café. Musée des Arts et Traditions Populaires, Paris.

Skate with Black Butter · Raie au Beurre Noir

	UK	US	
180–240 g	6–8 oz.	6–8 oz.	skate in one piece
			flour
			salt
			freshly ground black pepper
30 g	1 oz.	2 Tb	butter
	1 tsp	1 tsp	capers
	1 tsp	1 tsp	wine vinegar
	4	4	sprigs parsley
			oil

Serves 1

Preheat the oven to gas mark 2, 300° F.

Sprinkle both sides of the skate with flour seasoned with salt and pepper. Melt the butter in a frying pan over low heat and fry the skate gently on both sides, pressing it down with a spatula if it bends or warps. Cook until the flesh is opaque and white throughout, about 15 minutes. Transfer the skate to an oven dish and keep warm in the oven while you finish the sauce.

Turn the heat up under the frying pan and tip the butter round the pan until it burns brown (not black, as the name of the sauce implies). Add the capers and vinegar, and more salt and pepper as necessary. Cook for 1 minute longer, pour over the skate and serve immediately, garnished with fried parsley and accompanied by steamed potatoes.

To fry the parsley:

Wash the sprigs and dry them thoroughly. In a small pan, heat 1½ in. of oil until it is hot enough to crisp a cube of bread in 1 minute. Fry 3–4 sprigs at a time for about 2 minutes, removing them as soon as they start to turn dark green. Drain on a paper towel. Sprinkle with salt and reheat briefly in the oven if necessary before serving with the skate.

Cold Salmon in Aspic ·
Saumon Froid en Aspic

The salmon is baked in aluminium foil in the oven, then cooled and decorated. Wrapping the fish in foil and baking it in the oven prevents the flesh from drying out and all the juices are retained. Fish of any size may be cooked in this way; one is not restrained by the size of a fish kettle or dish, only by the size of the oven.

This method of cooking was, of course, unknown until recently. Large fish were poached in court-bouillon in a fish kettle, which small households were (and are) unlikely to have. Cooking in foil is therefore a welcome innovation, especially as it is both simple and easy.

	UK	US	
	1	1	salmon, weighing about 3 kg/ 6 lb., cleaned, but with head and tail left on
60 g	2 oz.	½ stick	butter
	1	1	lemon
			salt, pepper
			aspic powder or gelatin

garnish:

		cucumber, fresh tarragon leaves or chives, parsley, lemons and mayonnaise (see recipe, p. 97)

Serves 10

Set the oven to gas mark 5, 375° F. Melt the butter and measure out a length of double aluminium foil, longer than the fish and large enough to enclose it. Pour the butter down the middle of the foil lengthwise, where the salmon will lie. Place the salmon on the foil and pour more butter inside and on top of the fish. Squeeze lemon juice inside and outside the fish and sprinkle it with salt and pepper. Fold the foil securely round the fish, making sure that the juices cannot escape. Place on a baking sheet with slightly raised edges, so that it can hold 2 tablespoons of water as well.

In order to fit the salmon in the oven it may be necessary to place the fish at an angle on the baking sheet. Place the head of the fish towards one of the back corners of the oven; the tail can, if necessary, bend upwards against the door of the oven with no ill effect. Bake for 1 hour. Remove from oven, open up the foil and let the salmon cool for 15 minutes.

Probably the best place for the following procedure is beside the kitchen sink. Put a small bowl in the sink and tip the fish juices into it. Strain the juice through a sieve and put it into the refrigerator to cool.

Now carefully peel off the skin, removing fins and the brownish flesh which covers much of the pink flesh of the salmon. Turn the fish to the other side and repeat the operation. Place the fish, held in the aluminium foil, on a serving dish and very carefully slide the foil from under the fish or tear it away from the underside without damaging the flesh. Let it cool completely.

To decorate the fish, prepare the fish aspic first, then the cucumber, tarragon and parsley. First remove the butter from the fish liquid by skimming it off the top. Then stir 2 teaspoons aspic powder or 3 teaspoons gelatin into 150 ml/$\frac{1}{4}$ pint/$\frac{2}{3}$ cup of liquid. If necessary, add water to make up to this amount. Heat the liquid over simmering water until the powder or gelatin is completely dissolved, transfer to a bowl and put it to cool again in the refrigerator, remembering to use it before it sets. To hasten this process, place the bowl over another bowl filled with ice cubes and stir occasionally until it thickens.

In the meantime prepare the cucumber. Wash it but do not peel it. Slice it very finely, as fine as paper, so thin that you can see through the slices. It does not matter if some slices are not completely round, for the halves can be used as well.

If using tarragon, remove the leaves from the stalk and reserve. Separate parsley into small sprigs.

When the aspic has begun to set but is still liquid, brush some of it all over the fish with a pastry brush. Dip some slices of cucumber in the aspic and, starting at the tail end, arrange layers of slices to resemble fish scales. One can cover the entire fish in this way, or leave a gap and put parsley sprigs in the middle, with tarragon leaves or chives placed at intervals to resemble the bone structure. Remove the eye and fill the gap with a sprig of parsley. Brush with another layer of aspic and keep it cool in the refrigerator if it is a hot day. Remember that the aspic must be just liquid and the fish cold for this glazing to succeed.

Surround with more parsley, cucumber slices, lemon quarters and rosettes of mayonnaise.

' A few weeks later, when I went upstairs, the sun had already set . . . a sky of the same pink as the salmon that we should presently be ordering at Rivebelle reawakened the pleasure which I was to derive from the act of dressing to go out to dinner.'

IV, 143

Smelts and Gudgeon · Eperlans et Goujons

Smelts, like gudgeon, are freshwater fish but they live in the sea, only spawning in the rivers. They are small and transparent-looking and have a distinct smell of cucumbers when fresh.

		UK	US	
450 g		1 lb.	1 lb.	smelts or gudgeon
			2 scant	
430 ml		¾ pint	cups	oil, *or*
300 ml		½ pint	1¼ cups	oil and
90 g		3 oz.	¾ stick	butter
		1 tsp	1 tsp	salt
		2 Tb	2 Tb	flour
		1	1	lemon
		8	8	sprigs of parsley

Serves 2

Gut the fish, wash them and drain them well in a colander.

Set the oven to gas mark 3, 325° F.

Pour oil or a mixture of oil and butter into a frying pan to a depth of ¾ inch. Heat until it is hot enough to crisp a small cube of bread in 1 minute. If serving with fried parsley, fry the sprigs for 2 minutes each, drain on paper towels and keep hot in the oven.

Mix the salt and flour together and roll the fish lightly in this just before cooking. Fry a few at a time so that they are not crowded in the pan, over brisk heat, until they are brown and crisp (about 7 minutes), turning if necessary. Drain on a napkin or paper towel and keep warm in the oven.

Sprinkle with a little more salt and pepper and serve with lemon halves and fried parsley.

'With regard to smelt, I remember that the first time he asked me for them, he did so with his usual malicious kindness. "I should enjoy some fried smelt, Céleste. But I suppose you don't know how to prepare them?" he said, watching me with his little eyes to make sure. I was annoyed. I replied that of course I knew how, and indeed I went down to the fishmonger. When I saw those little fish, which made me think of tiny snakes, I asked myself all sorts of questions. What did one do with them? Did one gut them? . . .'

CA, 99, 100

The man from Prunier's: drawing by Sem.

Fillets of Sole with White Wine Sauce · Filets de Sole au Vin Blanc

	UK	US	
	1	1	sole/flounder weighing 400–500 g/1 lb. approximately, head off
200 ml	7 fl. oz.	1 scant cup	dry white wine
200 ml	7 fl. oz.	1 scant cup	water
	1	1	sprig thyme
	2	2	sprigs parsley
			juice of ½ lemon
	4	4	small shallots
75 ml	3 fl. oz.	7–8 Tb	double/heavy cream
	2	2	egg yolks
			salt, pepper
	6	6	crescents of puff pastry (see recipe. p. 156)

Serves 2

Proust's friend Mme Scheikévitch tells of being invited to Ciro's restaurant in 1916, where Proust did the ordering. '"Have you some nice fillets of sole done in white wine? some boeuf mode? some salad? and I would recommend a lovely creamy chocolate soufflé." He himself had a glass of water to help take his pills, and many cups of coffee.'

Letters

Skin and fillet the fish, making 4 fillets. Put the skin and bones into a saucepan with the wine and water, thyme, parsley and lemon juice. Boil fairly briskly for 10 minutes.

Peel and chop the shallots very finely and place in a frying pan with the fillets folded in three on top of them. Strain the fumet/fish stock over the fillets, cover, and simmer very gently until the fish turns white throughout. This takes about 5 minutes. Take the fillets out carefully with a slotted spoon or wire spatula and place in an oven-proof dish. Cover lightly and keep warm in a very low oven, gas mark 1, 275° F.

Reduce the fumet/fish stock by simmering another 10 minutes. Strain into a small saucepan and add the cream. Cook for a further 5 minutes until the sauce begins to thicken. Whisk the egg yolks and add to the sauce. Stir with a wooden spoon over low heat until the sauce is thickened further and coats the back of the spoon. To avoid curdling, stir constantly and keep the heat low. Season with salt and pepper and strain over the fillets.

Garnish with puff pastry crescents and serve with steamed potatoes, lightly sprinkled with parsley, or with plain rice.

Grilled/Broiled Sole · Sole Grillée

	UK	US	
	4	4	Dover sole/flounder
	1 Tb	1 Tb	flour
	½ tsp	½ tsp	salt
			pepper
75 g	2½ oz.	5 Tb	butter
	2	2	lemons

Serves 4

Have the heads cut off and the fish skinned. Lightly dust with the flour, salt and pepper. Dot with butter and grill/broil gently until the flesh is white all through (about 4–6 minutes each side). Serve with lemon quarters.

Fried Sole · Sole Frite

	UK	US	
	4	4	Dover sole/flounder
	1 Tb	1 Tb	flour
	½ tsp	½ tsp	salt
			pepper
300 ml	½ pint	1¼ cups	oil
	2	2	lemons

Serves 4

Prepare the fish as above and lightly dust with flour, salt and pepper. Heat the oil until a small piece of bread crisps in 1 minute. Fry the fish one at a time, turning once. Keep warm in a low oven.

Trout · Truite Farcie aux Epinards

Trout can be prepared in many ways. Simple grilling/broiling or frying is usual. They are often poached in red or white wine, or 'au bleu' (the live fish is stunned by a blow on the head, cleaned quickly and plunged into a boiling court-bouillon for a few minutes).

In the following recipe the trout is poached in cider, then stuffed with a spinach and shallot mixture and glazed with a tarragon-flavoured cream sauce.

	UK	US	
	4	4	trout, cleaned, heads left on
120 g	4 oz.	1 cup	cooked chopped spinach (see recipe, p. 91)
	3	3	small shallots or 1 medium onion
30 g	1 oz.	2 Tb	butter
430 ml	$\frac{3}{4}$ pint	2 scant cups	dry cider
	1 Tb	1 Tb	chopped fresh tarragon (or $\frac{1}{2}$ Tb dried)
			salt, pepper
150 ml	$\frac{1}{4}$ pint	$\frac{2}{3}$ cup	double/heavy cream

Serves 4

In the dining-room at the hotel in Balbec: "'I say, Chief, those little trout don't look at all bad, do they? We must ask Aimé to let us have some. Aimé, that little fish you have over there looks to me highly commendable: will you bring us some, please, Aimé, and don't be sparing with it."

III, 376

Finely chop the shallots or onion and fry gently in half the butter until golden. Add the spinach, mix with the shallots and cook until any moisture has evaporated. Taste for seasoning, remove from the heat and reserve.

In a frying pan large enough to hold the trout, melt the rest of the butter and pour in the cider. Bring to the boil, then turn the heat down to low, so that it barely simmers. Cook two trout at a time for 2 minutes each side, just long enough to loosen the skin. Trout need very little cooking and become fragile, so use a spatula in each hand to remove them to a board or dish. Reserve the cooking liquid. Carefully remove and discard the skin from both sides. Stuff the cavities with the spinach and shallot mixture and lay the fish alternately head to tail in a shallow oven dish, from which they will be served.

Set the oven to gas mark 4, 350° F. Add the tarragon, salt and pepper to the cooking liquid and reduce to approximately 115 ml/4 fl. oz./$\frac{1}{2}$ cup by cooking over high heat for about 10 minutes. Add the cream and cook for about 15 minutes over medium heat until the sauce thickens. In the meantime heat the fish through in the oven for 10 minutes and before serving pour the sauce over them, leaving their heads and tails uncovered. Decorate each trout with a tarragon leaf.

Serve with steamed or puréed potatoes if desired, and flat mushrooms (see recipe for Duck with Red Wine, p. 68).

Whiting · Merlans en Colère

'En colère' refers to a particular style of presenting the cooked whiting. The fish seems to be angry because it is biting its own tail.

1 whiting per person
flour
salt
pepper
oil for shallow frying
lemon
parsley

Choose whiting weighing approximately 230 g/½ lb. each and get the fishmonger to skin them (optional) and fasten their tails between their teeth with a wooden peg or piece of toothpick. The fishmonger should know how to do this and even be willing, if he is given enough advance notice. If not, have a try at accomplishing this preparation of the whiting yourself.

Sprinkle the fish all over with flour, salt and pepper. Heat the oil until it crisps a small piece of bread in 1 minute. Set the oven to gas mark 1, 275° F. Fry the fish one at a time for about 3–5 minutes on each side and keep them warm in the oven. Serve with quarters of lemon and sprigs of parsley (or fried parsley – 1 minute in hot oil, see recipe for Skate in Black Butter, p. 48).

Whiting 'en colère'. *La Cuisine d'aujourd'hui* by Urbain Dubois, 1900.

Meat

Entrecôte, Rump or Sirloin Steak

Steaks are best cooked with high heat, using either the kitchen grill/broiler, or a grilling or frying pan, if outside, using a charcoal fire in a hibachi or barbecue grill. The following recipe calls for a grilling pan; the French trade names are 'Monogrill' and 'Cousances grill'.

2 steaks weighing 125–175 g/4–6 oz. each
1 Tb oil
juice of $\frac{1}{2}$ lemon
freshly ground black pepper
salt

Serves 2

Marinate the steaks in the oil, lemon juice and pepper for 1 hour or so. This helps to tenderize the meat and enhances its flavour. Heat a grilling pan over medium heat for a few minutes before cooking the steaks. When ready, place the steaks diagonally across the ridges of the pan and press down a little with a spatula. Now turn them through a right angle and press down again. This will produce the desired cross-hatch grill marks. Turn the steaks over and repeat the process. Cook for 2–2$\frac{1}{2}$ minutes on each side if you like them medium rare. With the addition of a sprinkle of salt and pepper, they are ready to eat. Serve with fried potatoes.

Marcel, gazing out of his window in Paris, notices amongst other sights and sounds: 'In a butcher's shop, between an aureole of sunshine on the left and a whole ox suspended from a hook on the right, an assistant, very tall and slender, with fair hair and a throat that escaped above his sky-blue collar, was displaying a lightning speed and a religious conscientiousness in putting on one side the most exquisite fillets of beef, on the other the coarsest parts of the rump, placing them upon glittering scales surmounted by a cross, from which hung down a number of beautiful chains, and – albeit he did nothing afterwards but arrange in the window a display of kidneys, steaks, ribs – was really far more suggestive of a handsome angel who, on the day of the Last Judgment, will prepare for God, according to their quality, the separation of the good and the evil and the weighing of souls.'

IX, 180

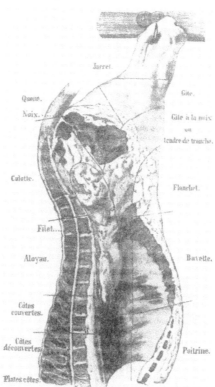

Side of beef: naming the parts.
La Cuisine d'aujourd'hui by Urbain Dubois, 1900.

Tournedos Rossini

This famous classical dish was invented by Gioacchino Rossini, the composer, who used to dine at Magny's restaurant in Paris with a group of writers, Sainte-Beuve, Dumas, George Sand, Turgenev and the Goncourt brothers among others.

Gioacchino Rossini: caricature by Hippolyte Mailly.

	UK	US	
	2	2	tournedos (fillets of beef or tenderloin) weighing 125–175 g/4–6 oz. each
	2	2	slices of bread the same size as the tournedos
175 g	6 oz.	2 cups	button mushrooms
120 g	4 oz.	1 stick	butter
75 ml	3 fl. oz	6 Tb	madeira
			a little flour
	2	2	slices of foie gras, the same size as the tournedos (if foie gras is not available, pâté de foie gras may be substituted)
40 ml	1½ fl. oz.	3 Tb	single/light cream
			salt and freshly ground pepper
			squeeze of lemon juice
	1	1	truffle, thinly sliced

Serves 2

'*At half-past two I had a meal of two tournedos and didn't leave a scrap, a plate of fried potatoes, twenty times the amount Félicie makes for us, cream cheese, Gruyère, two croissants and a bottle of beer.*'

Correspondance avec sa mère

Marinate the slices of foie gras in the madeira for 1–2 hours.

Wash the mushrooms. Discard the stalks and slice them thinly. Sauté slowly in half the butter for 5 minutes, taking them off the heat before they start to crisp. Squeeze a little lemon juice on them.

Cut the crust from the slices of bread and fry them in the rest of the butter, on both sides, until crisp. Keep warm in the oven at gas mark 2, 300° F.

Drain the foie gras slices, reserving the madeira, pat dry with paper towels, flour lightly and sauté in butter for about ½ minute on each side. Keep warm in the oven. Pâté de foie gras will not need cooking but may be put into the oven, with its marinade, for a few minutes to warm through.

Sear the meat in the same frying pan that was used for the bread. Turn it quickly if you like the meat underdone; cook for about 3 minutes on each side if you prefer it medium rare. Place in the oven to keep warm.

Deglaze* the pan with the madeira in which the foie gras has been marinating. Add the mushrooms, truffle, salt, pepper and cream. Let it bubble for a few minutes.

Now assemble the tournedos: first the croûton with a spoonful of the sauce on it, then the steak, a slice of foie gras and the rest of the sauce.

* Deglazing is an essential procedure in French cooking. It helps to achieve a sauce that will complement the meat. The method is as follows: after roasting, sautéing or frying meat, remove most of the fat, if there is any, from the pan by tilting it and lifting off the fat with a spoon. Add water, wine or whichever liquid is specified in the recipe, and over medium heat scrape the pan well, gathering up the browned bits and juices left in the pan.

Bœuf à la Bourguignonne

	UK	US	
1·8 kg	4 lb.	4 lb.	stewing beef – leg of beef, shin, shoulder, skirt (chuck and bottom round)
	2	2	onions, sliced
	2 Tb	2 Tb	oil
			sprig of thyme
300 ml	½ pint	1¼ cups	red wine
225g	½ lb.	½ lb.	fat pork or bacon
	24	24	small onions
	2 Tb	2 Tb	oil or fat
	2 Tb	2 Tb	flour
230 ml	8 fl. oz.	1 cup	red wine
	2	2	cloves of garlic, crushed
			salt, pepper
			bouquet garni (parsley, thyme, bayleaf)
350 g	¾ lb.	¾ lb.	mushrooms (button mushrooms preferred)
30 g	1 oz.	2 Tb	butter (to fry mushrooms in) chopped parsley to garnish

(onions, sliced / oil / sprig of thyme / red wine — } marinade)

Serves 8

Trim the meat and cut it into 1¼-inch cubes. Place in a bowl with the oil, onions, thyme and red wine and leave to marinate for 6–8 hours or overnight.

Next day, remove the tips and root ends of the small onions. Pour boiling water over them and let them steep for 5 minutes. Drain and peel them when cool enough to handle.

Fry the bacon lightly until just beginning to brown. Remove, leaving the fat in the pan; cut the bacon into small pieces and reserve. Brown the small onions in the bacon fat over medium heat. Remove and reserve.

Drain the beef, reserving the marinade. Pat the meat dry. Make sure it is at room temperature, to facilitate cooking. To save time, two frying pans can be used. Sear the meat over high heat in oil or fat (including the bacon fat that the small onions were fried in). As the pieces brown, remove them with a wire spatula or slotted spoon to a heavy casserole. When all the meat is brown, deglaze each frying pan with 115 ml/4 fl. oz./½ cup of the strained marinade. Over low heat scrape the sides and bottom of the pans for a few minutes, obtaining a dark-brown stock.

Stir in the flour and let it brown for 2 minutes.

Add the stock from the frying pans, the rest of the marinade, the extra red wine, garlic, salt, pepper, bouquet garni and extra stock if needed to cover the meat. Slowly bring to the boil and simmer over low heat for 2 hours. Add the bacon and onions after 1 hour.

If using button mushrooms, wash them and keep them whole, only removing the stalks. If only larger mushrooms are available, wash and slice them. Fry gently in butter for a minute or two until they lose a little of their moisture. Add the mushrooms to the casserole after 2 hours of cooking.

Test meat for tenderness after 2 hours of cooking. Turn the stew into a serving dish and sprinkle with chopped parsley. A cabbage and potato purée (see recipe, p. 87) or steamed potatoes go well with this, with a salad to follow.

Bœuf Stroganof

	UK	US	
1½ kg	3 lb.	3 lb.	fillet tails or fillet of beef (tenderloin tips)
	3	3	medium onions, sliced
350 g	¾ lb.	¾ lb.	mushrooms, washed and sliced
125 g	4 oz.	1 stick	butter
300 ml	½ pint *or* 2 cartons	1¼ cups	sour cream
30 g	1 oz.	4 Tb	flour
			freshly ground black pepper
	¾ tsp	¾ tsp	salt
	½ tsp	½ tsp	nutmeg (optional)
	½ tsp	½ tsp	mace (optional)

Serves 8

'Grande armoire à glace' – ancestor of the refrigerator. *La Cuisine d'aujourd'hui* by Urbain Dubois, 1900.

Cut the meat into strips approximately 3 inches long and ¾ inch wide. Cut with the grain of the meat. Put them on a wooden board and sprinkle with flour and ground pepper. Flatten the strips with a wooden mallet or large heavy spoon. Sauté the onions in a third of the butter in a large heavy casserole, turning often until they are golden in colour.

Wash and slice the mushrooms and fry them separately for two or three minutes in a third of the butter, until some of the moisture has evaporated. Add them to the onions in the casserole over very low heat.

Sear the meat in the frying pan in the rest of the butter over fairly high heat, turning quickly and adding to the casserole as the strips are cooked. They will cook very quickly, in only a minute or two. Deglaze the pan with a tablespoon of warm water, raising the heat and scraping the pan well. Some nice brown gravy will appear if you have seared the meat well. Add to the casserole and season with salt and more pepper.

Heat the sour cream, nutmeg and mace in a separate saucepan over low heat and stir into the meat just before serving. The sour cream will curdle if it is allowed to boil.

Serve with plain boiled rice (see recipe, p. 158).

Cold Spiced Beef with Carrots · Bœuf Mode

This dish is generally served cold, in which case it is necessary to start preparations the day before. It may, however, also be served hot.

	UK	US	
2·3 kg	5 lb.	5 lb.	top rump/rump roast, topside or silverside/boneless chuck
1 kg	2¼ lb.	2¼ lb.	cracked veal bones
	1	1	calf's foot, split, if available, *or*
	2	2	pigs' feet, split, and a piece of pork rind
	4 Tb	4 Tb	oil or lard
		2 large	onions
			onion skin
900 g	2 lb.	2 lb.	carrots
	2	2	cloves of garlic, crushed
	1 Tb	1 Tb	salt
			freshly ground black pepper
55 ml	2 fl. oz.	¼ cup	brandy
200 ml	8 fl. oz.	1 cup	dry white wine
	1	1	bayleaf
	1 tsp	1 tsp	dried thyme
	3	3	sprigs parsley
			large sliver of orange peel
2 litres	3½ pints	2 quarts	water or veal stock
			juice of ½ lemon
	3	3	egg whites

Serves 8

Note: the veal bones, calf's foot, pigs' feet and pork rind all have gelatinous qualities and will help the stock to jell completely naturally. Add the onion skin if it is a brown colour, for it will give colour to the stock.

Preheat the oven to gas mark 1, 275° F. Wipe the meat with a damp cloth. Rinse the veal bones and the calf's foot (or pigs' feet and pork rind). Scrape and trim half the carrots. Pick out a long one about an inch in diameter and slice the remainder. Insert a sharp, thin, long-bladed knife through the middle of the meat lengthwise; withdraw it and push in the carrot so that, when the meat is cooked and carved, each piece will have a slice of carrot in the centre of it.

In a large, heavy, flameproof casserole, brown the onions in oil or lard. Add the meat and sear it with the onions, turning it to brown it all over. (If the onions and meat are browned thoroughly, this will colour the stock naturally.) Ignite the brandy and pour it over the meat. When the flames die down, pour in the wine and let it bubble for 2 minutes. Then add the veal stock or water and the sliced carrots, garlic, herbs, orange peel, salt and pepper, and the veal bones and calf's foot (or pigs' feet and rind). Add more stock or water if necessary so that the meat is nearly covered.

Slowly bring to the boil and skim off scum as it appears on the surface. Then seal the casserole with foil and put the lid on. Cook in the oven for $3\frac{1}{2}$–4 hours, turning the meat occasionally. At this point check that the meat is tender, as it will harden up when cool. (If the dish is to be served hot, now is the time to slice the meat and serve it with the rest of the carrots boiled in some of the strained stock.)

Carefully lift the meat out of the casserole and leave it to cool. Then place in a covered dish and leave in the refrigerator overnight.

Reduce the stock by simmering it, uncovered, on top of the stove for $\frac{1}{2}$ hour, helping to ensure a jelly that will set. Strain through a fine sieve into a bowl; add lemon juice, cover, and chill overnight in the refrigerator. Discard the bones, vegetables and herbs.

Next morning, remove the layer of fat from the top of the stock. Scrape and slice the remaining carrots, and cook them in a third of this stock until tender. Drain the carrots, reserving the stock, and leave them to cool.

Combine the two portions of stock in a pan, leaving behind the sediment that has settled at the bottom of the bowl. Reheat slowly and taste for seasoning.

Beat the egg whites with a fork until foamy and pour on top of the stock. Simmer for 10 minutes. The egg whites will lift all the remaining sediment from the stock, and by straining it through cheesecloth you will achieve a jelly that is a 'transparency'! The stock should now be cooled and allowed 5–6 hours in the refrigerator to set again.

Slice the meat and arrange it on a large serving dish. Glaze the slices with a little softened jelly and sprinkle chilled jelly, cut into small cubes, around the edge. Garnish the dish with carrots and several sprigs of fresh parsley or watercress.

Serve with a bowl of green salad.

'Lisa la charcutière': lithograph (detail) by Bellanger from Zola's *Le Ventre de Paris*, 1879.

Grilled/Broiled Kidneys with Cognac Sauce · Rognons au Cognac

Kidneys need very little cooking, to ensure that they remain pink inside, very tender, and mild-tasting: 10 minutes for the large kidneys, 7 minutes for the small ones.

	UK	US	
	1	1	veal kidney per person, if small (about 100 g/¼ lb. each) *or*
	½	½	veal kidney per person, if large (about 200 g/½ lb. each)
			oil
			salt, pepper
15 g	½ oz.	1 Tb	butter
	2 Tb	2 Tb	cognac
125 ml	4 fl. oz.	½ cup	double/heavy cream
	20	20	juniper berries, crushed
			bunch of watercress to garnish

Remove the fat and membrane from around the kidneys and, keeping them whole, cut away the hard fat underneath. If the kidneys are large, stick 2 skewers through them cross-wise, so that they remain flat during the cooking. Turn on the grill/broiler, brush the kidneys with a little oil, sprinkle with salt and pepper and grill/broil the top for just 5 minutes. Melt the butter in a frying pan over medium heat and add the kidneys; sprinkle with crushed juniper berries and cook for 2 minutes. Turn down the heat, add the cognac and set alight. Remove the kidneys immediately to a warm place. Deglaze the pan with a tablespoon of water, scraping the pan well. Add the cream and season the sauce if necessary with more salt and pepper. Remove the skewers, if used, and pour the sauce over the kidneys. Garnish with watercress.

Roast Leg of Lamb or Mutton · Gigot Rôti

'. . . a roast leg of mutton, because the fresh air made one hungry and there would be plenty of time for it to "settle down" in the seven hours before dinner.'

I, 94

April is the time of year when the new season's lamb is available and at its most delectable. In France, the lambs from Paulhac (Gironde) and the *prés salés* (salt meadows) of Brittany are much favoured.

Small legs of lamb can be roasted with little seasoning for a reasonably short time (18 minutes per 450 g/1 lb. at gas mark 6, 400° F.). This will ensure that the meat is pink in the centre, for those who enjoy the meat this way; longer roasting time is required for well done meat (22 minutes per lb. at the same heat).

Legs of lamb weighing more than 3 kg/6 lb. can be marinated in either red or white wine (as preferred) for a few hours or overnight and roasted at a lower temperature for a longer time (25 minutes per 450 g/1 lb. at gas mark 5, 375° F.). Mutton has not been generally available for a number of years.

It is advisable to turn and baste the meat often during the cooking.

Paris butcher's shop, about 1900.
Photo Roger-Viollet.

The meat can be flavoured with garlic or not, as preferred, slivers of garlic being inserted in the leg of lamb before roasting. It can be garnished with vegetables added to the roasting pan during the last hour of cooking, such as flageolet beans, or white haricot beans, previously soaked overnight and cooked 1 hour, or with whole small onions or peeled potatoes.

The following recipe is for what is generally considered a large leg of lamb in the UK; legs of lamb in the USA usually weigh more and should cook longer.

	UK	US	
2·3 kg	5 lb.	5 lb.	(approx.) leg of lamb
			½ lemon
230 g	½ lb.	½ lb.	onions or shallots
	6	6	sprigs of thyme
			salt, pepper
230 ml	8 fl. oz.	1 cup	red wine
			bunch of watercress to garnish

Serves 8

Set the oven to gas mark 6, 400° F. Trim some of the fat from the leg, rub with the half lemon and sprinkle with salt and pepper. Place in a roasting pan.

Chop the onions or shallots finely and put them over and around the leg. Put the thyme on the leg also. Add 3 tablespoons water to the pan and pour on half the wine.

Roast, turning and basting every ¾ hour, replacing the onion and thyme on top of the leg, for 1¾ hours, when the meat should be well done. Shorten the cooking time by half an hour if the meat is preferred pink in the centre.

Remove the leg to a carving board or dish and let it stand for a few minutes while you make the gravy. The meat firms up and this makes the carving easier.

To make the gravy, add 115 ml/4 fl. oz./½ cup water to the roasting pan and, over medium heat, scrape the sides and bottom of the pan into the juices and simmer for 5 minutes. Spoon off the fat, add the rest of the wine, let it bubble, and strain the gravy into a pre-heated sauceboat.

Serve with steamed potatoes (see recipe, p. 90) and a béarnaise sauce (see recipe, p. 96) if desired. Garnish with watercress.

Grilled Lamb Cutlets · Côtelettes d'Agneau Grillées

2 cutlets per person
oil
lemon juice
salt
freshly ground black pepper
béarnaise or choron sauce (see recipes, p. 96)

Trim the cutlets of some of their fat and marinate them in oil and lemon juice for an hour. Preheat the grill pan/broiler and cook the cutlets for 7–10 minutes on each side. Sprinkle with salt and pepper and serve with the desired sauce.

Sweetbreads · Ris de Veau

Used in Bouchées à la Reine and Chicken Financière recipes.

	UK	US	
120 g	¼ lb.	¼ lb.	sweetbreads
	½ tsp	½ tsp	salt
15 g	½ oz.	1 Tb	butter
			squeeze of lemon juice
			salt, pepper

Soak the sweetbreads in cold water for 2–3 hours to remove all the blood, changing the water if necessary. Drain, and place in a saucepan with water and salt. Bring slowly to the boil and cook for 5 minutes. Drain, and when cool enough to handle, trim off any cartilage and other inedible bits, but do not remove the filament that surrounds them.

They may be cooked at this stage, but if there is time it is a good idea to press them, between two pieces of greaseproof paper with a weight on top. This helps to break down the fibres so that they will not shrink or curl up when cooking.

Cut sweetbreads into small pieces approximately ¾ in. square. Fry these pieces in butter for 5 minutes, turning when brown. Sprinkle with salt, pepper and lemon juice.

Poultry and Game

Chicken Financière · Poulet Financière

	UK	US	
1·8 kg	4 lb.	4 lb.	chicken, dressed
	1–2	1–2	black truffles, fresh or conserved
	1	1	medium onion
	2	2	carrots
	3	3	sprigs of parsley
	2 Tb	2 Tb	chicken stock (or water)
230 g	½ lb.	½ lb.	button mushrooms
45 g	1½ oz.	3 Tb	butter
120 g	4 oz.	4 oz.	prepared sweetbreads (see recipe, p. 62)
120 g	4 oz.	4 oz.	chicken breast ⎫
60 g	2 oz.	6 Tb	fresh white breadcrumbs ⎪
	1	1	egg yolk ⎬ chicken quenelles
	1 Tb	1 Tb	double/heavy cream ⎪
			salt ⎭
			squeeze of lemon juice
			pepper
	3 Tb	3 Tb	madeira

Serves 4–5

If fresh truffles are available, peel off the rough skin, reserving the peelings. Slice thickly and sauté gently in a little butter for barely a minute – they must not dry out. Pour over a little madeira to cover, and keep warm. Tinned/canned truffles need no cooking, just warming up in madeira.

Melt two-thirds of the butter in a heavy casserole and lightly brown the chicken over medium heat. Set the oven to gas mark 3, 325° F. Finely chop the onions and parsley and coarsely grate the carrots. Cut off the mushroom stems and chop them, reserving the mushrooms themselves.

Remove the chicken from the casserole to a side dish, and brown the onions, parsley, carrots and mushroom stems, gently, in the casserole in the remaining butter.

Return the chicken to the casserole, sprinkle with salt and pepper, lay it on its side and pour over the stock. Cover with a lid and cook for 1¼–1½ hours, turning the chicken to the other side after 20–30 minutes, and basting and turning breast side up for the final 45 minutes.

Prepare the chicken quenelles. Bone and skin the chicken breast and pound it in a mortar with a pestle or mince/grind in the liquidizer. Add the breadcrumbs (made with 2 thin slices white bread, crumbed in the liquidizer) and pound together until well mixed. Add the egg yolk, salt and cream, stir well and chill in the refrigerator for half an hour. Then shape into small balls and poach in barely simmering water for 10 minutes, turning once. Remove with a wire spatula or slotted spoon and keep warm.

Wash the mushrooms and sauté them in 15 g/½ oz./1 Tb of butter for 2–3 minutes until they have lost some of their moisture. Sprinkle with a squeeze of lemon juice. Keep warm. Heat the sweetbreads gently in butter and keep warm.

When it is cooked, remove the chicken to a serving dish. Carve it into pieces or keep it whole, as desired. Garnish with the sweetbreads, cut into small pieces, quenelles, mushrooms and truffles, and keep warm in a low oven.

Strain the juices and vegetables through a sieve into a saucepan, rubbing through as much of the vegetables as possible. Add the truffle peelings and/or liquid, the madeira they were heated in, and the remaining madeira, and simmer fairly briskly for about 15 minutes until the sauce is well reduced and thickened. Strain it over the chicken and serve.

'M. de Guermantes having declared (following upon Elstir's asparagus and those that were brought round after the financière *chicken) that green asparagus grown in the open air, . . . "ought to be eaten with eggs . . ."'*

VI, 268

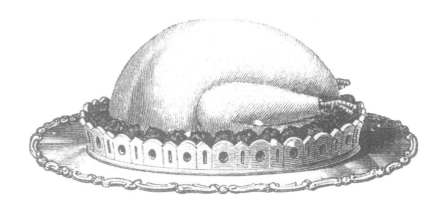

Boiled Chicken · Poule au Pot

Similar to a *petite marmite* or *pot au feu*. A boiling chicken is stuffed and simmered for a long time with veal knuckle and vegetables. The chicken and veal are then served up with some of the broth and freshly cooked vegetables.

	UK	US	
2·1 kg	4½ lb.	4½ lb.	boiling fowl, dressed (approx. weight)
1 kg	2 lb. 3 oz.	2 lb. 3 oz.	veal knuckle (approx. weight)
	3	3	turnips
	4	4	carrots
	3	3	onions
	3	3	leeks
	3	3	sprigs of thyme ⎫ tied in
	3	3	sprigs of parsley ⎬ a bouquet
	1	1	bayleaf ⎭ garni
	1 Tb	1 Tb	salt
			pepper

stuffing:

230 g	½ lb.	½ lb.	pork, such as shoulder
120 g	¼ lb.	¼ lb.	ham
	2	2	shallots
	3	3	slices white bread (crusts off) soaked in milk and squeezed dry
	1 Tb	1 Tb	chopped parsley
			salt, pepper
	1	1	egg, beaten
			the chicken liver (optional)

Serves 6

Cut the pork and ham into cubes. Skin and roughly chop the shallots. Mince/grind the pork, ham, chicken liver (if used) and shallots together, using the medium-hole plate of the mincer/grinder.

Mix together well with the bread, parsley, salt, pepper and beaten egg.

Stuff the chicken with this stuffing. Sew up the opening with needle and buttonhole thread or thin string.

Peel the turnips, scrape the carrots and slice them lengthwise. Cut off the root end of the onions but leave them whole and unpeeled. Trim the leeks, wash them well, and tie them in a bundle with string.

Place the veal knuckle, chicken, giblets, vegetables and bouquet garni in a very large *marmite*/stockpot or saucepan and nearly cover with cold water.

Bring to the boil over medium heat. It will take about half an hour to come to the simmering point and at this stage be ready to take off any scum that rises to the top. A nylon tea strainer with very fine mesh is the best tool for this, though a slotted spoon will also do the job.

The heat must be very low, so that the soup just barely shudders. Cover loosely with a lid so that some of the steam can escape. Cook for 3½ hours more, adding the salt and pepper in the last hour.

Discard the giblets and the vegetables, which will have overcooked. The broth may be served as soup (like a *petite marmite*) or reserved for another use.

Serve the chicken and veal with some of the stock and with freshly cooked leeks and carrots.

Mme Proust wrote to her son in 1890 that his father was indisposed, but that he was well enough to enjoy one of his favourite dishes, poule au pot.

Letters

Stock-pots, from *The Royal Cookery Book* by Jules Gouffe, 1868.

Roast Chicken · Poulet Rôti

	UK	US	
	I	I	chicken, 1·5–2 kg/3½–4 lb. dressed
	½	½	lemon
			salt
			freshly ground black pepper
30 g	1 oz	2 Tb	softened butter
	1–2	1–2	sprigs fresh tarragon *or*
	1 tsp	1 tsp	dried tarragon
	I	I	small onion, skinned and halved

Serves 6

Preheat the oven to gas mark 4, 350° F.

Rub the skin of the chicken with the cut side of the lemon and sprinkle the inside with salt and pepper. Insert half the softened butter under the skin from the neck end, together with 10–12 tarragon leaves, pushing it down over the breast and thighs with your fingers. Sprinkle the entire chicken with salt and pepper, and place the onion inside. Spread the rest of the butter over the chicken and place in an oven dish, breast side down, with 1 tablespoon of water. Roast for 45 minutes and then turn the bird breast side up and roast for another hour, basting occasionally. When the chicken is cooked the legs can be moved easily.

May be served hot or cold.

'*We used always to return from our walks in good time to pay Aunt Léonie a visit before dinner. In the first weeks of our Combray holidays, when the days ended early, we would still be able to see . . . a fiery glow which, accompanied often by a cold that burned and stung, would associate itself in my mind with the glow of the fire over which, at that very monemt, was roasting the chicken that was to furnish me, in place of the poetic pleasure I had found in my walk, with the sensual pleasures of good feeding, warmth and rest.*'

I, 181

Brillat-Savarin, the philosopher of the kitchen, makes a distinction between application and genius: 'Cooks are made but a rôtisseur is born'. From *L'Art de bien manger* by E. Richardin, 1910.

Duck with Red Wine · Canard au Vin Rouge

	UK	US	
	1	1	duck, dressed, weighing about 2 kg/4–5 lb. with giblets
430 ml	¾ pint	2 cups	red Bordeaux
125 g	4 oz.	4 oz.	bacon or fat pork
125 g	4 oz.	4 oz.	large flat mushrooms (about 6), *or*
230 g	½ lb.	½ lb.	button mushrooms
	1	1	small onion
			½ lemon
			salt, pepper
	½ tsp	½ tsp	thyme
	1 Tb	1 Tb	oil
			bunch of watercress for garnish

Serves 4

Set the oven to gas mark 6, 400° F. Remove the little glands (sacs) from the tail, because their strong taste might permeate the duck. Rub the skin of the duck with half a lemon.

Peel the onion, cut it in half and place it inside the duck to give it flavour. Prick the fatty sides of the duck with a fork. This helps the fat to run out and eventually to crisp the skin. Salt and pepper the duck inside and out and place in a roasting pan, breast side down. This will help the meat to stay moist. Pour 2 tablespoons of wine over the duck and set to roast.

Wash the gizzard, heart and neck and put in a saucepan with cold water to cover; simmer while the duck is cooking. Reserve the liver for another use (see recipe for Foie Gras, p. 26).

After ¾ hour prick the skin of the duck again and turn it breast side up, draining off any fat that has appeared. Baste with more wine and cook for a further half hour. Drain off the fat again and pour some wine inside the duck. The wine will flavour it even though some is poured away with the fat.

In the meantime, cook the bacon until it crisps and, when cool, cut it into 1-inch pieces.

Trim the stalks of the flat mushrooms, lay them in a flat oven dish and sprinkle with salt, pepper, thyme and 1 tablespoon of oil. If using the button mushrooms, wash and slice them and cook in 60 g/2 oz./½ stick of butter for a minute or two until some of the moisture has evaporated. Reserve.

The duck needs to roast for 1½ hours. A quarter of an hour before the end of cooking time, drain off the remaining fat (reserving it for another use*) and

---

* Duck fat keeps well in the refrigerator for 2–3 weeks and is an excellent and tasty fat for frying and sautéing. To conserve, cool the fat in a bowl, then chill in the refrigerator. When it has congealed, turn it out into another bowl, separate the juices (which will be in the bottom) from the fat. The juices can be used to flavour a sauce or gravy.

add the rest of the wine. The duck is cooked when you can move the legs easily.

Remove the duck from the oven, carve it into pieces and arrange it on an oven dish. Reset the oven to gas mark 4, 350° F., and replace the duck to crisp the skin further.

Using the roasting pan to finish the sauce, add the bacon and 3 tablespoons of the giblet stock to the wine and juices in the pan. Simmer over low heat for 5 minutes, scraping the sides and bottom of the pan well. Pour the sauce over the duck, garnish with the mushrooms and decorate with watercress.

'"Saint-Loup with helm of bronze,"
said Bloch, "have a piece more of this
duck with thighs heavy with fat, over
which the illustrious sacrificer of birds
has spilled numerous libations of red
wine."'

IV, 102

Wild duck: illustration from *Le Journal de la décoration*. Musée des Arts et Traditions Populaires, Paris.

Roast Goose · Oie Rôtie

	UK	US	
	1	1	goose, dressed, with giblets, weighing about 4 kg/9 lb.
			½ lemon
			salt, pepper
230 ml	8 fl. oz.	1 cup	red wine
15 g	½ oz.	1 Tb	butter

stuffing:

	UK	US	
	2	2	onions, finely chopped
230 g	½ lb.	½ lb.	mushrooms
60 g	2 oz.	½ stick	butter
230 g	½ lb.	½ lb.	pure pork sausage meat*
350 g	¾ lb.	¾ lb.	minced/ground pork*
175 g	6 oz.	6 oz.	breadcrumbs
	2	2	eggs
	1 Tb	1 Tb	raisins
			clove of garlic, chopped fine
			salt, pepper
			pinch of thyme
	2 Tb	2 Tb	cognac
	2 tsp	2 tsp	arrowroot (optional for thickening the gravy)
			parsley for garnish

Serves 8

Set the oven to gas mark 6, 400° F.

Wash the gizzard, heart and neck and place in a saucepan with cold water; bring to the boil and simmer while the goose cooks.

Melt 60 g butter in a frying pan, add the onions and cook over medium heat until tender and golden in colour. Chop the mushrooms finely and add to the onions. Fry for 3 minutes so that they lose some of their moisture and add the sausage meat and the minced/ground pork. Stir and cook for another 7 minutes. Put the rest of the stuffing ingredients into a bowl and add the cooked mixture. Mix well and stuff the goose. Close the opening with toothpicks or sew with strong thread.

Rub the goose with the lemon and sprinkle with salt and pepper. Prick the fatty sides with a fork to allow the fat to run out during the cooking.

Place in a roasting pan, breast side down (to keep the meat moist) and pour over it half the wine. If the goose seems very fatty, place it on a rack in the roasting pan, so that it need not lie in its own fat.

Roast for 45 minutes, basting once or twice. Drain off the fat that has accumulated, reserving this for another use, and turn the goose breast side up. Baste with more wine, prick the fatty sides again and cook for another hour or

---

* If the goose appears to be very fatty, replace the sausage meat and minced/ground pork with 350 g/¾ lb. minced/ground veal and add another 60 g/2 oz./½ stick butter to the stuffing.

hour and a quarter, basting occasionally. When you can move the legs easily, the goose is tender enough to eat. Place it on a serving dish and leave for 10 minutes in a warm place, so that the flesh firms up and carving will be easier.

Make the gravy by pouring off the fat from the roasting pan and adding 15 g/½ oz./1 Tb of butter, the rest of the wine and 230 ml/8 fl. oz./1 cup of the giblet stock. Cook over medium heat, scraping the sides and bottom of the pan well. Strain into a little saucepan and check for seasoning. Add salt and pepper if necessary, and simmer until needed. The gravy may be thickened with the addition of a paste made by mixing 2 teaspoons of arrowroot with 2 tablespoons of cooled giblet stock. Stir into the gravy and heat through, until it thickens.

Carve the goose, disjointing the legs and wings, and cutting thin slices across the breasts. Cut the meat free from the breast bone and replace the slices so that the whole bird can go to the table. Remove the toothpicks or string from the opening. Serve with gravy and garnish with parsley sprigs. Vegetables such as sauerkraut, red cabbage with braised chestnuts, glazed onions or a purée of potatoes are suggested as accompaniments.

'Jean was still too young to realize that before a wonderful roast goose could be set upon the table, superbly limbed and shining with gravy so that his mouth watered with innocent desire, it had been necessary to catch a terrified creature, to struggle with it, to wring its neck and to drain away oceans of blood down the kitchen sink. When he heard cluckings and the flapping of frightened wings in the yard he still believed that it was only the cock being punished, but not hurt, for misbehaving with the hens.'

Jean Santeuil, 113

Braised Turkey à la Normande · Dindonneau à la Normande

More often than not, small turkeys with a rich stuffing are served in Normandy.

	UK	US	
2½ kg	5½ lb.	5½ lb.	dressed turkey (approx. weight)
60 g	2 oz.	½ stick	butter
	1	1	medium onion
	1	1	medium carrot
	3	3	sprigs of parsley
	4 Tb	4 Tb	double/heavy cream
	2 Tb	2 Tb	Calvados

marinade:

	UK	US	
300 ml	½ pint	1¼ cups	dry white wine
	2	2	sprigs of thyme

stuffing:

	UK	US	
			liver and heart of the turkey
230 g	½ lb.	½ lb.	pure pork sausage meat
	1	1	medium onion
	5	5	slices of white bread
	6	6	cooked prunes
	2 Tb	2 Tb	raisins
			salt, pepper
	1 Tb	1 Tb	Calvados
	2 Tb	2 Tb	double/heavy cream

'It required some exceptional circumstance nevertheless to induce him [Aimé, the general manager of the Rivebelle restaurant] one day to carve the turkey-poults himself. I was out, but I heard afterwards that he carved them with a sacerdotal majesty, surrounded, at a respectful distance from the service-table, by a ring of waiters.'

VIII, 318

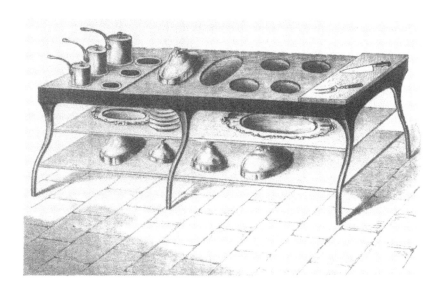

Serving table for hotels and restaurants, kept hot by steam or hot water. *La Cuisine d'aujourd'hui* by Urbain Dubois, 1900.

Marinate the turkey breast side down in a bowl with the wine and thyme overnight.

To make the stuffing mince/grind the turkey liver and heart and the onion together. Cut the crusts from the bread and crumb in the liquidizer. Mix all the stuffing ingredients together and stuff the turkey's body cavity and the neck end. Fasten the openings with toothpicks or sew with strong thread.

Chop the onion and parsley and coarsely grate the carrots. In a heavy casserole, large enough to fit the turkey, melt the butter, add the onion, parsley and carrots and brown them a little. Also lightly brown the turkey, turning it on to both sides and on its back. Strain the marinade over it.

Set the oven to gas mark 3, 325° F. With the turkey on its side, cover the casserole and cook for $2\frac{1}{2}$–3 hours, turning the turkey at 45-minute intervals first to the other side, then breast side down and finally breast side up.

Lift the turkey on to an oven-proof serving dish and return to the oven while making the sauce. Strain all the juices and vegetables in the casserole into a small saucepan and rub most of the vegetables through. Skim off the fat. Bring the sauce to the boil and cook over low heat for 10–15 minutes until the sauce is reduced to about 300 ml/$\frac{1}{2}$ pint/$1\frac{1}{4}$ cups. Add the cream and Calvados, simmer for 2 minutes and pour over the turkey.

Serve with chestnut purée or potato purée (see recipes, pp. 89 and 90).

Grouse. *La Cuisine d'aujourd'hui* by Urbain Dubois, 1900.

'*It was of some feast in the Gospels portrayed with a mediaeval simplicity and an exaggeration typically Flemish that one was reminded by the quantity of fish, pullets, grouse, woodcock, pigeons, brought in dressed and garnished and piping hot by breathless waiters who slid over the polished floor to gain speed and set them down on the huge carving table where they were at once cut up . . .*'

V, 127

Grouse · Coq de Bruyère

	UK	US	
	$\frac{1}{2}$ or 1	$\frac{1}{2}$ or 1	grouse
15 g	$\frac{1}{2}$ oz.	1 Tb	butter
	1 Tb	1 Tb	madeira
			salt, pepper
	1	1	slice of bread
			watercress to garnish

Serves 1

Set the oven to gas mark 6, 400° F.

Cut the crusts from the bread. Melt half the butter in a frying pan and fry the bread on both sides until crisp. Melt more butter and pour inside and over the grouse. Sprinkle with salt and pepper. Place the grouse, breast side down, in the roasting pan and add a little madeira. Roast for 15 minutes. Turn the grouse breast side up, baste, and roast for another 10–15 minutes.

To serve, place the grouse on top of the croûtons in a serving dish and keep warm in the oven, lowering the temperature to gas mark 1, 275° F. Make a sauce by deglazing the roasting pan with a little water or stock over medium heat, scraping the pan well and adding a little more madeira. Let it bubble, taste for seasoning and serve separately. Garnish the grouse with watercress.

Decorative panel from a Paris butcher's shop.

'But though the Duchess disliked entertaining on a grand scale at Réveillon, she equally disliked being there alone. . . . Letters were written calling the faithful to the colours. "The blue room is waiting for you. Boniface has now got a range on which he can concoct lièvre à l'allemande *just as you like it."'*

Jean Santeuil, 439

Hare à l'Allemande · Lièvre à l'Allemande

A saddle of hare is often roasted whole for this dish, but in the following recipe the hare is first jointed into 8 pieces.

	UK	US	
	I	I	hare, drawn and dressed (there is no need to reserve the blood)
	2	2	medium onions
	I	I	sprig of thyme
	10	10	juniper berries, crushed
			salt
			ground black pepper
430 ml	¾ pint	2 cups	dry white wine
	2 Tb	2 Tb	cognac
	2 Tb	2 Tb	madeira
	2 Tb	2 Tb	oil
230 g	½ lb.	½ lb.	carrots
	3	3	sprigs of parsley
45 g	1½ oz.	3 Tb	butter or duck fat
300 ml	½ pint	1¼ cups	double/heavy cream or sour cream (with a squeeze of lemon juice if the former is used)
			redcurrant jelly

Serves 8

Cut the hare into 8 pieces, if desired, or leave whole, and remove as much as possible of the sinews and second skin – the thin membrane that covers the flesh. Slice half the onions thinly and put them with the hare in a bowl; add the thyme, juniper berries, pepper, wine, cognac, madeira and oil. Marinate overnight or at least 4 hours, turning occasionally.

Chop the carrots, remaining onions and parsley finely, and lay in the bottom of a large roasting pan. Set the oven to gas mark 6, 400°F. Drain off the marinade and reserve. Place the sliced onions from the marinade with the vegetables in the roasting pan. Dry the pieces of hare and lay on top of the vegetables; spread them with butter or duck fat and sprinkle with salt and pepper. Cover the pan loosely with aluminium foil and roast for 1½ hours, basting occasionally with the strained marinade and turning the pieces of hare over every ½ hour. Uncover for the last 20 minutes, to brown the hare lightly.

Remove the hare to a serving dish and put it back into the oven to keep warm, having lowered the temperature to gas mark 4, 350°F. Strain off the juices and vegetables from the roasting pan, reserving the juices and putting the vegetables into a separate oven dish. Bake the vegetables for 15 minutes more while preparing the sauce.

Add the cream to the reserved juices and boil for 10 minutes to thicken; add the lemon juice if necessary, and pour over the hare. Serve with the vegetables, a dish of buttered noodles and redcurrant jelly to accompany.

Truffled Partridge · Perdreaux Truffés

	UK	US	
	2	2	partridges
	1	1	truffle
	2 Tb	2 Tb	duck, goose or chicken fat
30 g	1 oz.	2 Tb	butter
	2	2	vine leaves
			salt, pepper
	1 Tb	1 Tb	cognac
	3 Tb	3 Tb	stock
			watercress to garnish

Serves 2

24 hours before serving, slice the truffle thinly and insert 4 small slices under the breast skin of the partridges. Place the rest of the truffle inside the birds, with the fat. Leave in the refrigerator or a cool place for the flavour of the truffle to permeate the partridges.

Set the oven to gas mark 6, 400° F. Smear butter over the partridges, sprinkle with salt and pepper, and tie a vine leaf over the breasts.

Place the partridges, breast side down, in an oven dish, legs resting on the side of the pan, and pour over the cognac. Roast for 30 minutes, turning breast side up after 15 minutes, and baste. Remove the string.

Place the partridges in a serving dish and keep warm in the oven. Add 3 tablespoons of stock or water to the pan juices, scrape the sides and bottom of the pan, sprinkle over with salt and pepper, and cook over medium heat for 2 minutes. Strain into a sauceboat. Garnish with watercress.

A dish of partridge: illustration from *La Cuisine artistique* by Urbain Dubois.

75

Stuffed Pheasants · Faisans Farcis

	UK	US	
			a brace of pheasant, cock and hen, dressed but not trussed
stuffing:			
175 g	6 oz.	6 oz.	chicken livers
	2	2	pheasant livers
175 g	6 oz.	6 oz.	mushrooms
	1 Tb	1 Tb	goose or duck fat; if not available, use butter
30 g	1 oz.	2 Tb	butter
	2 Tb	2 Tb	chopped shallots or onions
	1 Tb	1 Tb	chopped walnuts
	1 Tb	1 Tb	chopped parsley
			salt, pepper
	1 Tb	1 Tb	cognac
	2	2	slices pork fat, to bard the pheasants
	2 Tb	2 Tb	madeira, for the sauce

Serves 4

Dinner at Mme de Guermantes: M. de Grouchy says,

' "*Well as a matter of fact, I have had quite a good bag. I shall take the liberty of sending the Duchess six brace of pheasants tomorrow.*"

' *An idea seemed to flicker in the eyes of Mme de Guermantes. She insisted the M. de Grouchy must not give himself the trouble of sending the pheasants. And making a sign to the betrothed footman with whom I had exchanged a few words on my way from the Elstir room:*

' "*Poullein,*" *she told him,* "*you will go tomorrow and fetch M. le Comte's pheasants and bring them straight back – you won't mind, will you, Grouchy, if I make a few little presents. Basin and I can't eat a whole dozen by ourselves.*"

' "*But the day after tomorrow will be soon enough,*" *said M. de Grouchy.*

' "*No, tomorrow suits me better,*" *the Duchess insisted.*

'*Poullein had turned pale; his appointment with his sweetheart would have to be missed.*'

VI, 242

Detail of 'Count Tessin's Dachshund': painting by Jean-Baptiste Oudry, 1740. National Museum, Stockholm.

Set the oven to gas mark 6, 400° F.

Melt the duck or goose fat in a frying pan and cook the chicken and pheasant livers gently until they begin to brown. Remove from the pan and leave to cool.

Melt 1 tablespoon of butter in a frying pan and cook the onions or shallots until they are golden. Wash and chop the mushrooms, add them to the shallots and cook them for a minute or two until they lose some of their moisture.

Chop the pheasant and chicken livers very small, put them in a bowl and add the rest of the stuffing ingredients, moistening with the cognac.

Stuff the pheasants and close the openings with toothpicks or sew with strong thread. Tie pieces of pork fat to each breast and place the pheasants, breast side down, in the roasting pan (to keep the flesh moist), resting their legs on the side of the pan. Smear the backs with butter and add 2 tablespoons of water to the pan.

Roast for $\frac{1}{2}$ hour, then re-set the oven to gas mark 4, 350° F., and turn the pheasants breast side up. Baste. Cook for another 20 minutes, take off the pork fat, baste again and let the skin brown slightly for 10 minutes. The total cooking time for an average-sized pheasant is 1 hour.

Place the pheasants in a serving dish and keep warm. Pour off most of the fat that has accumulated in the pan, sprinkle in half a tablespoon of flour, and on top of the stove, over low heat, stir, scraping the sides and bottom of the pan well. Add a tablespoon or two of water if there are not enough juices in the pan to make the sauce. Add 2 tablespoons of madeira, simmer for a minute, taste for seasoning and strain into a sauceboat.

Quail · Cailles sur Canapés

	UK	US	
	1–2	1–2	quail, cleaned (livers reserved)
60 g	2 oz.	$\frac{1}{2}$ cup	white grapes
	1–2	1–2	slices of white bread, crusts removed
			butter
			salt, pepper

Serves 1

Cut the bread to the same size as the quail. Fry gently in butter both sides until they become crisp golden croûtons.

Halve and seed the grapes and mix half of them with the quail livers. Stuff the quail with this mixture, and close the opening with toothpicks.

Set the oven to gas mark 8, 450° F. Smear the quail with butter, sprinkle with salt and pepper and place on a rack in a roasting pan.

Roast for 25 minutes, lowering the oven temperature to gas mark 4, 350° F., after 15 minutes and basting at the same time.

Remove the toothpicks and serve on the croûtons, garnished with the remaining grapes, halved, seeded and sautéed in a little butter.

Rabbit with Mustard, Onion and Cream Sauce · Lapin à la Cauchoise

	US	US	
1 kg	2 lb.	2 lb.	rabbit pieces
	1 Tb	1 Tb	flour
			salt, pepper
15 g	½ oz.	1 Tb	butter
	2 Tb	2 Tb	Dijon mustard
	1	1	large onion
	1 Tb	1 Tb	dry white wine
230 ml	8 fl. oz.	1 cup	double/heavy cream

Serves 4

Sprinkle the rabbit pieces with flour, salt and pepper. Melt the butter in a frying pan and fry the rabbit over medium heat until lightly browned. Remove to a casserole dish and keep warm.

Finely slice the onion and brown it in the same frying pan used to brown the rabbit, adding more butter if necessary.

Spread mustard all over the rabbit and add the browned onions and a tablespoon of white wine. Cover and simmer very gently over low heat (use a simmering mat if necessary), turning the rabbit pieces over once, or bake in an oven set to gas mark 3, 325° F., for 1 hour. A quarter of an hour before end of cooking time, stir in the cream and taste for seasoning. Serve with steamed potatoes (see recipe, p. 90).

'*I had extorted from Françoise, who though opposed to war was cruel, that she would cause no undue suffering to the rabbit which she had to kill, and I had had no report yet of its death. Françoise assured me that it had passed away as peacefully as could be desired, and very swiftly. "I have never seen a beast like it; it died without uttering a word; you would have thought it was dumb." Being but little versed in the language of beasts I suggested that the rabbit had not, perhaps, a cry like the chicken's. "Just wait till you see," said Françoise, filled with contempt for my ignorance, "if rabbits don't cry every bit as much as chickens. Why, they are far noisier." *'

III, 78–9

Shop sign of 'Le lapin agile'. Musée de Montmartre, Paris.

Venison · Chevreuil

Venison can be the reason for preparing a special dinner. It is worth while to accompany the venison with a madeira sauce made with redcurrant jelly, pears stuffed with bilberries (cranberries can be substituted), with creamed mushrooms and some buttered noodles on the side. All the recipes for these follow; please read all the instructions before starting preparations.

	UK	US	
	8	8	médaillons of deer* (1 kg/ 2 lb. 3 oz.)
230 ml	8 fl. oz.	1 cup	red wine
30 g	1 oz.	2 Tb	butter
	2 Tb	2 Tb	marc or cognac (optional)

Serves 8

Médaillons need little cooking, so it is advisable to prepare the sauce and the garnishes for this dish in advance.

Marinate the médaillons in the red wine for 2 hours.

Drain off the wine and pat the médaillons dry. Melt the butter in a frying pan over medium heat. Before it starts to brown, add the médaillons and brown both sides well. Cook a few at a time, and keep them warm in an oven, gas mark 1, 275° F. When all the médaillons have been browned, return a few at a time to the pan, pour over some of the marc or cognac and set alight (optional). Return to the oven dish and keep warm in the oven, so that they continue to cook gently all the way through (approximately 20 minutes).

Before serving, remove the strings and pour over the sauce.

Redcurrant Sauce

Follow the recipe for madeira sauce (p. 98), adding 2 tablespoons of redcurrant jelly with the lemon juice and madeira. Stir well.

Bilberries:

	UK	US	
125 g	4 oz.	1½ cups	bilberries (or cranberries)
	2 Tb	2 Tb	sugar
	1 Tb	1 Tb	water

Wash the berries and put them in a saucepan with the sugar and water. Cook over low heat for 20 minutes, stirring occasionally. A few of the berries will pop as they cook, so remove promptly from the heat, making sure that most of the berries remain whole. Put aside.

---

* Médaillons are made with the meat cut from the saddle of a small deer. If possible, ask your butcher to do this, otherwise buy a half saddle and cut the meat carefully off the bone. Trim these 'fillets' of all skin and sinews, lay together and shape into a larger 'fillet'. Tie with 8 pieces of string at intervals and slice into 8 médaillons, approximately 1¼ in. thick. If the (real) fillets are on the underside of the half saddle which you have purchased, include these in the larger 'fillet'.

Pears:

8 little cooking pears (such as Conference)
water
2 Tb red wine
2 Tb sugar

Peel the pears, leaving the stalk on. Place in a saucepan with the sugar, wine and enough water to nearly cover. Cook over medium heat for 20–30 minutes until tender.

Remove from the syrup and when cool enough to handle cut them across about a third of the way from the top. Cut a thin slice from the bottom, so that they can sit upright in an oven dish. With a demi-tasse or small teaspoon, scoop out the core and some of the pear and fill the hollow with bilberries. Use the top of the pear as a little hat partially covering the berries. Spoon over some syrup and put aside until near serving time, when they should be re-heated briefly in the oven.

Barquettes:

Make a half of the pastry recipe on p. 114, leaving out the sugar and egg yolk and adding a pinch of salt and a little more water instead. Chill in the refrigerator for ½ hour. Take it out and let it soften a little, for 5–10 minutes. Flour a board or counter and roll out to ⅛-inch thickness, and line 8 barquette moulds. Prick with a fork.

Set the oven to gas mark 6, 400° F. Place small pieces of crushed aluminium foil on the pastry, so that it keeps its shape, and put the barquette moulds on a baking sheet. Bake for 20 minutes in all, removing the foil after 15 minutes. If the pastry has risen, press it back into shape with foil while it is still warm. Let it cool. Invert the pastries on to a cake rack.

Mushroom filling for barquettes:

	UK	US	
120 g	¼ lb.	¼ lb.	chanterelles or morel mushrooms, if available, or button mushrooms; *otherwise*
15 g	½ oz.	½ oz.	dried chanterelles or other mushrooms, soaked in cold water for 2 hours
15 g	½ oz.	1 Tb	butter
115 ml	4 fl. oz.	½ cup	double/heavy cream

Wash the mushrooms and remove the sandy end of each stalk. Slice them finely and fry gently in butter for 5 minutes or until they have lost some of their moisture and started to crisp. Add the cream, salt and pepper and simmer for 5 minutes. Pour into the barquettes just before serving, so that the pastry does not have time to get soggy.

Noodles:

	UK	US	
450 g	1 lb.	3¾ cups	flour
	3 Tb	3 Tb	extra flour for kneading
	2	2	large eggs
	½ tsp	½ tsp	salt
150 ml	¼ pint	⅔ cup	single/light cream*
	1 Tb	1 Tb	oil
30 g	1 oz.	2 Tb	butter, melted

Sieve the flour and salt into a bowl. Make a well in the flour, break in the eggs and add the cream. Stir with a wooden fork or spoon until all the flour is incorporated. Turn this rough dough on to a floured board and knead for 10 minutes, adding more flour if necessary, until a smooth, elastic dough is attained. Put in a plastic bag and chill in the refrigerator for an hour.

Divide the dough into 3 pieces. Flour a board or counter and roll out one piece very thin, adding more flour as necessary. Try to roll the piece into a large square shape (about 12 in. square) to facilitate the cutting of the noodles.

Now cut the noodles with a sharp knife, approximately to a width of $\frac{5}{16}$ in. Carefully gather them up from the board and drape them over the back of a chair for half an hour to dry a little.

Repeat with the rest of the dough. Wrap the noodles round the fingers, forming little nests, and leave covered with a slightly damp cloth until needed.

Bring a saucepan of salted water to the boil, add a tablespoon of oil and the noodles and cook for 3–4 minutes until just tender – 'al dente'. Drain, and toss in the melted butter. Serve sprinkled with freshly ground black pepper.

Serve the venison on a large platter with the sauce poured over, and garnished with the pears. Serve mushroom barquettes, noodles and extra bilberry or cranberry sauce on the side.

* The inclusion of cream makes these noodles delicious.

Woodcock · Bécasse

	UK	US	
	I	I	woodcock, trussed, head left on, but innards left inside except for gizzard
			salt, pepper
	2 Tb	2 Tb	white wine
	I	I	slice of white bread, same size as woodcock
30 g	I oz.	2 Tb	butter
	I tsp	I tsp	lemon juice
	I Tb	I Tb	cognac
			straw potatoes and watercress for garnish

Serves 1

Set the oven to gas mark 7, 425° F.

Trim the crust off the bread. Melt 1 tablespoon of butter in a frying pan over medium heat and fry the bread on both sides until it is a crisp and golden croûton. Place in an oven dish.

Sprinkle the woodcock with salt and pepper and smear with soft butter. Place on its side in a roasting pan and pour over 2 tablespoons white wine. Roast for 15 minutes, turning and basting after 10 minutes.

Remove from the oven. Cut some backbone away, with kitchen shears, from the tail end, removing the innards at the same time. Discard the backbone but reserve the innards. Return the woodcock to the oven. Chop the innards and spread them on the croûtons. Put in the oven while the woodcock finishes cooking for another 5 minutes. Total cooking time is 25 minutes. The flesh will be pink.

Place the woodcock on the croûton and keep it warm. Add the lemon juice and cognac to the roasting pan and heat briefly on top of the stove, scraping the pan well. Strain into a sauceboat, or pour straight on to the woodcock.

Garnish with straw potatoes and watercress.

Woodcock. *La Cuisine d'aujourd'hui* by Urbain Dubois, 1900.

Vegetables and Salads

Artichokes · Artichauts

1 large artichoke per person
lemon
salt
olive oil

Cut the stem of the artichoke down to 1 in. and peel it. Remove some of the tough outer leaves and, with a sharp knife or kitchen scissors, cut off the points of the remaining leaves, trimming $\frac{1}{2}$ in. off the top leaves.

Wash under running water and squeeze plenty of lemon juice all over the outside and inside of the artichoke, to prevent the flesh from blackening.

Bring a saucepan of water to the boil, with 2 teaspoons of salt and 1 tablespoon olive oil. Boil the artichoke for 20–30 minutes or until an outside leaf pulls off easily. Drain for a few minutes upside-down.

Artichokes cooked in this manner with lemon juice and olive oil are very flavourful and do not need to be served with a sauce. But hollandaise sauce is delicious with them, or lemon butter, if served hot, and a vinaigrette sauce if served cold. See recipes for sauces, pp. 96–102.

From the street cries of Paris: '. . . the motives were beginning, even at this early hour, to become confused, a vegetable woman, pushing her little hand-cart, was using for her litany the Gregorian division:
A la tendresse, à la verduresse,
Artichauts tendres et beaux,
Arti . . . chauts
although she had probably never heard of the antiphonal, or of the seven tones that symbolize four the sciences of the quadrivium and three those of the trivium,'

IX, 154

Asparagus · Asperges

	UK	US	
1·5 kg	3½ lb.	3½ lb.	asparagus
	1½ tsp	1½ tsp	salt for each litre/1¾ pints/1 quart of water

Serves 4–6

Remove the pointed leaves up to 4 cm (1½ inches) from the tip and peel or scrape the lower half. Wash well and tie into bundles. Cook in plenty of boiling salted water for 20 minutes. If you have a narrow, tall saucepan to cook the asparagus in upright, with stems down, take advantage of it.

Drain well and serve on a folded napkin.

Asparagus Sauce

The tender part of the cooked asparagus can be puréed by rubbing them through a fine sieve or by putting them through the blender. Stir in a little butter and some cream, to taste, and you have a wonderfully delicate sauce to accompany chicken, slices of ham or lightly poached eggs.

Five more sauces to accompany asparagus are: hollandaise, mousseline or vinaigrette sauce, clarified/drawn butter, or lemon butter (see pp. 96–102).

'. . . but what fascinated me would be the asparagus, tinged with ultramarine and rosy pink which ran from their heads, finely stippled in mauve and azure, through a series of imperceptible changes to their white feet, still stained a little by the soil of their garden-bed: a rainbow-loveliness that was not of this world. I felt that these celestial hues indicated the presence of exquisite creatures who had been pleased to assume vegetable form, . . .'

I, 163–4

French Beans with Vinaigrette Sauce · Haricots Verts Vinaigrette

	UK	US	
450 g	1 lb.	1 lb.	French beans
			vinaigrette sauce (see recipe, p. 102)
	1 tsp	1 tsp	mixed chopped *fines herbes* (chervil, parsley, tarragon)

Serves 4

Cut off the stem end of the beans and wash. Steam in a vegetable steamer for 12 minutes, or until tender but still crunchy.

Prepare the vinaigrette sauce. Rinse the beans in cold water as soon as they are tender. Place them in a serving dish, sprinkle with the *fines herbes* and pour the vinaigrette sauce on them. Leave to marinate for at least ½ hour. Serve at room temperature.

' "Very well, I'm off, but I never want anything again for our dinners except what we've heard cried in the street. It is such fun. And to think that we shall have to wait two whole months before we hear: 'Haricots verts et tendres, haricots, v'là l'haricot vert.' How true that is: tender haricots; you know I like them as soft as soft, dripping with vinegar sauce, you wouldn't think you were eating, they melt in the mouth like drops of dew." '

IX, 167

Cardoons with Marrow ·
Cardons à la Moelle

Another dish that Françoise cooked for Marcel's family: 'cardoons with marrow, because she had never done them for us in that way before . . .'

I, 94

Cardoons belong to the thistle genus and are closely related to the artichokes. Their taste is similar to that of artichokes although they are more like celery in appearance. They are grown for their stalks.

	UK	US	
	I	I	bunch of cardoons (about 1 kg/ 2 lb.)*
	4	4	marrow bones, 3–4 in., previously simmered for 20 minutes
	2 Tb	2 Tb	flour
115 ml	4 fl. oz.	½ cup	water
	1 Tb	1 Tb	salt
			juice of 1 lemon
15 g	½ oz.	1 Tb	butter
			salt, pepper

Serves 4

Trim the stalks and cut them into 4-in. lengths. Wipe them clean. A plastic picnic knife will not blacken the stalks. If using a metal knife, wipe them immediately with lemon juice.

Mix the flour and water together in a little bowl and pour this mixture into an enamel or earthenware saucepan, half full of water. Bring to the boil, add the juice of half the lemon, a tablespoon of salt and the cardoon stalks. Bring to the boil again and simmer for half an hour or until tender. Drain the stalks in a plastic or enamel colander or strainer, rinse with cold water, remove any tough outside strings, and place in an oven dish.

Set the oven to gas mark 5, 375° F. Dot the cardoons with butter, sprinkle with salt and pepper and additional lemon juice and bake for 10 minutes.

Remove the marrow from the bones, place this on top of the cardoons, heat for a further 5 minutes and serve.

Traditionally, this dish requires *sauce moelle*, a madeira sauce (see recipe, p. 98) with marrow, but the above recipe is less rich and the flavour of the cardoons is better preserved.

Cardoon. *Larousse gastronomique.*

* Cardoon stalks blacken if they come into contact with metal, so it is advisable to use an earthenware or enamel-lined saucepan and to boil them in a flour-and-water mixture, with lemon juice, which will keep them white.

Cabbage and Potato Purée ·
Purée de Choux et de Pommes de Terre

	UK	US	
900 g	2 lb.	2 lb.	cabbage
1100 g	2½ lb.	2½ lb.	potatoes
45 g	1½ oz.	3 Tb	butter
	3 Tb	3 Tb	milk (approximately)
			salt, pepper
			grated nutmeg

Serves 8

Steam the unpeeled potatoes in a vegetable steamer for 25 minutes. Remove the tough outer leaves of the cabbage, cut into quarters and remove the hard core. Chop coarsely.

When the potatoes are cooked, steam the cabbage for 20 minutes. Peel the potatoes when cool enough to handle, and rub through the fine mesh of the mouli food mill into a saucepan. Rub the cabbage through the medium mesh of the food mill on top of the potatoes. Heat the butter and milk together until warm, add to the cabbage-and-potato mixture, with salt, pepper and nutmeg. Beat hard with a wooden spoon over low heat, adding more milk if necessary to obtain a light and fluffy purée. Taste for seasoning.

Creamed Carrots · Carottes à la Crème

	UK	US	
450 g	1 lb.	1 lb.	carrots
	1 tsp	1 tsp	salt
	1 tsp	1 tsp	sugar
15 g	½ oz.	1 Tb	butter
230 ml	8 fl. oz.	1 cup	double/heavy cream
			freshly ground black pepper

Serves 4

' "*Voilà des carottes, à deux ronds la botte.*" "*Oh!*" *exclaimed Albertine, "cabbages, carrots, oranges. All the things I want to eat. Do make Françoise go out and buy some. She shall cook us a dish of creamed carrots. Besides, it will be so nice to eat all these things together. It will be all the sounds that we hear, transformed into a good dinner.*" '

IX, 166–7

Scrape the carrots, slice them across into rounds or, if you prefer, cut them lengthwise into four and then cut into 2½-in. lengths. Put into a saucepan and barely cover with cold water. Add the salt and sugar and cook, uncovered, over medium heat until tender. This should take between 20 and 30 minutes, depending on the age and type of the carrots. Strain off the remaining water, if any (there should be very little), and add the butter to the saucepan. Toss the carrots in the butter for a few minutes; add the cream and simmer for 5 minutes until the cream thickens. Pour into a vegetable dish and sprinkle with freshly ground black pepper.

Peas with Onions and Lettuce ·
Petits Pois à la Française

	UK	US	
1 kg	2 lb.	2 lb.	fresh peas in the pod (or half this quantity of frozen peas)
	12	12	small onions*
	1	1	round lettuce heart
	2	2	spring onions/scallions
30 g	1 oz.	2 Tb	butter
	1 tsp	1 tsp	salt
			pepper

Serves 4

Pod the peas, if fresh, and soak in a bowl of cold water if not using immediately. Pour boiling water over the onions, let them steep for 5 minutes, drain and peel when cool enough to handle. Discard some of the outer leaves of the lettuce and wash it, keeping it whole.

Melt the butter in a heavy saucepan and add the onions. Cook over medium heat, shaking the pan occasionally until the onions are slightly brown all over. Add the peas, salt and pepper. Place the lettuce heart in the centre, cover saucepan tightly and turn the heat to low.

Cook for 20–25 minutes until the peas are tender. Frozen peas will lose some of their unnatural greenness, which will only improve the appearance of the dish.

Chop the spring onions/scallions finely and sprinkle over the peas a few minutes before serving.

* If small onions are not available, use 1 medium onion, chopped.

Detail from an etched glass shop sign in Paris (20 Avenue Ledru-Rollin).

Chestnut Purée · Purée de Marrons

	UK	US	
450 g	1 lb.	1 lb.	chestnuts
150 ml	¼ pint	⅔ cup	milk
150 ml	¼ pint	⅔ cup	water
	½ tsp	½ tsp	salt
			pepper
	1 Tb	1 Tb	chopped onion
15 g	½ oz.	1 Tb	butter

Serves 3–4

' "*You are going to have a* purée *of chestnuts, I need say no more than that . . ."* '

VI, 248

Slit half the chestnuts down one side and drop into boiling water for 10 minutes. Drain and peel off the outer shell and inner skin as quickly as you can while they are still hot. Once cold, the skin begins to adhere to the nut again, so keep the chestnuts in hot water until you are ready to peel them. Repeat with the remaining chestnuts.

Put the chestnuts into a saucepan. Add the milk, water, onion, salt and pepper, bring to the boil, and simmer very gently until they are tender. This will take ½ hour to 1 hour depending on the freshness of the chestnuts. Add more liquid if necessary.

Rub the chestnuts and any remaining liquid through the fine mesh of the mouli food mill twice and stir in the butter. Taste for seasoning and, if the purée is too liquid, reduce it over medium heat, stirring, until it has the consistency of puréed potatoes.

Fried Potatoes · Pommes Frites

Proust's friend Paul Morand tells of a visit to Proust's apartment, in 1917, when 'Céleste was ordered to open the cider and make pommes frites *in my honour.'*

Journal d'un attaché d'ambassade

Fried potatoes are a perfect accompaniment to grilled steaks or grilled chicken.

	UK	US	
400 g	14 oz.	14 oz.	potatoes
550 ml	1 pint	2½ cups	oil
			salt

Serves 2

Peel the potatoes and cut them into neat thin sticks. Put them into a bowl of cold water for at least ½ hour so that the starch can soak out. Drain, and pat thoroughly dry with a tea cloth or paper towels. Heat the oil for several minutes. It is hot enough to start frying when a small cube of bread crisps in it in 1 minute. Fry the potatoes in batches, so that they do not crowd the frying pan and the temperature of the oil does not drop. When they are crisp and golden, drain well and sprinkle with salt. Keep the chips warm while frying the next batch.

Steamed Potatoes · Pommes à la Vapeur

	UK	US	
1.3 kg	3 lb.	3 lb.	potatoes
			salt water

Serves 8

Wash the potatoes well, but there is no need to peel them. Place in the top of a steamer, above a saucepan of boiling water. Cover, and steam for 20–25 minutes; the exact cooking time depends on the size of the potatoes. Peel them as soon as they are cool enough to handle. Sprinkle with salt before serving.

Particularly suitable for serving with fish and meat dishes that have an accompanying sauce.

Pommes à l'anglaise are generally boiled but may also be steamed as above.

Boiling or steaming the potatoes in their skins helps to ensure that a potato which tends to flake or become floury keeps its shape during cooking. This method is also less wasteful and more nutritious than the more traditional way of first peeling them and shaping them into olives.

'Françoise a colonel with all the forces of nature for her subalterns . . . would be stirring the coals, putting the potatoes to steam . . .'

1, 163

Potato Purée · Purée de Pommes

A good accompaniment to many dishes, especially those with a sauce.

	UK	US	
1600 g	3½ lb.	3½ lb.	potatoes
300 ml	½ pint	1¼ cups	milk
90 g	3 oz.	¾ stick	butter
	1 tsp	1 tsp	salt
	½ tsp	½ tsp	freshly ground black pepper
	½ tsp	½ tsp	freshly grated nutmeg

Serves 8

Wash the potatoes, leaving them unpeeled, and steam for 25 minutes. As soon as they are cool enough to handle, peel them and rub them through the finest mesh of the mouli food mill. Bring the milk and butter to the boil, remove from the heat and pour on to the potatoes. Add salt, pepper and nutmeg and beat with a wooden spoon until a smooth and fluffy purée is obtained. Add more milk if a more liquid purée is desired, and taste for seasoning. Place in an oven dish and keep warm in a very low oven before serving.

Milk-vending machine in the Paris of 1900.

Detail of the kitchen at Illiers.
Photo Doisneau-Rapho.

Leaf Spinach · Epinards en Branches

	UK	US	
450 g	1 lb.	1 lb.	spinach
45 g	1½ oz.	3 Tb	butter
			freshly ground nutmeg
			salt, pepper

Serves 2–3

One of the dishes Françoise made for Marcel's family: '. . . spinach, by way of a change . . .'

I, 94

Tear the spinach from the stalks, wash it well and drain, leaving on some of the moisture. Melt the butter in a large saucepan, add the spinach and sprinkle with salt and pepper. Cook, uncovered, over medium heat for 5 minutes until the moisture has evaporated and the spinach begins to sauté. Place in a serving dish and sprinkle with nutmeg.

Spinach Purée with Cream · Purée d'Epinards à la Crème

same ingredients as above, plus
3 Tb double/heavy cream
4 fleurons (puff pastry crescents)

Serves 2–3

Cook as above, allow to cool, place on a board and chop finely. Return to the pan with a little freshly ground nutmeg and the cream. Stir together for 2 minutes over medium heat. Garnish with fleurons.

Stuffed Tomatoes I

Each version of this dish serves 4. If serving 8, it might be a good idea to use both versions, to give some variety and choice.

	UK	US	
	4	4	medium tomatoes
	5	5	thin slices of white bread
60 g	2 oz.	½ stick	butter
			salt
	1	1	small clove of garlic pushed through a garlic press (optional)
	1 Tb	1 Tb	chopped parsley

Cut out a small round from the tops of the tomatoes and scoop out the pulp with a teaspoon. Discard or reserve for another use. Drain the tomatoes upside-down for half an hour.

Remove the crusts from the bread and cut into very small (¼-in.) cubes. Melt the butter in a frying pan over medium heat, add the bread cubes (and garlic if desired) and fry until golden. Sprinkle with salt.

Set the oven to gas mark 4, 350° F. Sprinkle the insides of the tomatoes with a little salt and fill with the tiny croûtons mixed with chopped parsley, place in a shallow oven dish and bake for 10 minutes.

Stuffed Tomatoes II

4 medium tomatoes
2 thin slices of white bread, or 4 Tb fresh breadcrumbs
2 eggs
1 Tb oil
1 Tb chopped parsley
salt, pepper

Cut out a small round from the tops of the tomatoes and scoop out the pulp with a teaspoon. Sieve the pulp, reserving the juice. Drain the tomatoes upside-down for half an hour.

Boil the eggs for 10 minutes, strain, and cover with cold water. When cool, shell the eggs, remove the whites and reserve the yolks.

Remove the crusts from the bread, tear into small pieces and crumb it in the liquidizer. Rub the egg yolks through a sieve into a bowl, add the crumbs, tomato juice, oil, parsley, salt and pepper. Mix lightly with a fork.

Set the oven to gas mark 4, 350° F. Sprinkle the insides of the tomatoes with a little salt and fill with the stuffing. Place in a shallow oven dish and bake for 10 minutes.

'This rubicund youth, with his blunt features, appeared for all the world to have a tomato instead of a head. A tomato exactly similar served as head to his twin brother. . . . Tomato II shewed a frenzied zeal in furnishing the pleasures exclusively of ladies, Tomato I did not mind condescending to meet the wishes of certain gentlemen. . . . M. Bernard would accost the twin brother with: "Will you meet me somewhere this evening?" He at once received a resounding smack in the face. . . . In the end this treatment so disgusted him, by association of ideas, with tomatoes, even of the edible variety, that whenever he heard a newcomer order that vegetable, at the next table to his own, in the Grand Hotel, he would murmur to him: "You must excuse me, Sir, for addressing you, without an introduction. But I heard you order tomatoes. They are stale today." '

VIII, 1–2

Pineapple and Truffle Salad · Salade d'Ananas et de Truffes

It is pure ostentation to mix truffles with pineapple, but the following recipe is pleasant, though unusual. Pineapple and vinaigrette is refreshing and delicious.

1 pineapple
1–2 black truffles
vinaigrette sauce (see recipe, p. 101)
1 chicory/endive for garnish

Serves 6

'My mother was counting greatly upon the pineapple and truffle salad. But the Ambassador, after fastening for a moment on the confection the penetrating gaze of a trained observer, ate it with the inscrutable discretion of a diplomat and without disclosing to us what he thought of it.'

III, 42

Peel the pineapple, discard the hard core and cut into small cubes. Cut the truffles into fine julienne strips. Mix the pineapple and truffles with the vinaigrette sauce and allow to steep for at least an hour before serving. Arrange in a bowl surrounded with chicory/endive leaves.

Potato Salad · Salade de Pommes de Terre

Marcel reads of a dinner party at the Verdurins in an unpublished Goncourt Journal. ' "... I do not know many places in which a simple potato salad is made as it is here with potatoes firm as Japanese ivory buttons and patina'd like those little ivory spoons with which Chinese women sprinkle water over their new-caught fish." '

XII, 20

	UK	US	
700 g	1½ lb.	1½ lb.	potatoes – choose the waxy type
150 ml	¼ pint	⅔ cup	mayonnaise (use half amount of recipe, p. 97), *or*
150 ml	¼ pint	⅔ cup	vinaigrette sauce (see recipe, p. 101)
			salt, pepper
	1 Tb	1 Tb	chopped chives

Serves 4–5

Wash and steam the potatoes (see recipe, p. 90) in their skins for 20–25 minutes. Rinse with cold water and peel them when cool enough to handle. Leave to cool.

Cut them into ¾-in. cubes or slices. Sprinkle with salt and pepper and lightly stir in mayonnaise or vinaigrette, whichever is preferred. Sprinkle with chives just before serving.

Russian Salad · Salade Russe

This dish serves as a light luncheon course or a cold hors-d'œuvre.

	UK	**US**	
230 g	½ lb.	½ lb.	green beans
230 g	½ lb.	½ lb.	carrots
500 g	1 lb.	1 lb.	fresh peas in the pod, *or*
230 g	½ lb.	½ lb.	frozen peas
125 g	¼ lb.	¼ lb.	turnips (optional)
230 g	½ lb.	½ lb.	potatoes
300 ml	½ pint	1¼ cups	mayonnaise (see recipe, p. 97)
			juice of ½ lemon
			salt and freshly ground pepper

Serves 8

Peel and dice the carrots and the turnips, top and tail the green beans, and wash the potatoes. Pod the peas if necessary. First boil the potatoes in salted water until tender, then the turnips, carrots, green beans and peas. Be sure not to overcook the vegetables. Drain and rinse in cold water to refresh them. Peel and dice the potatoes and chop the beans into small lengths. Combine all the vegetables together and leave to cool. Just before serving, stir in the mayonnaise and lemon juice and season with salt and pepper.

Garnish with anchovy fillets, truffles, mushrooms or capers, or one of the following selections: 125 g/¼ lb. smoked salmon strips, 4 hard-boiled eggs, halved, and 8 teaspoons caviar or lumpfish caviar; or 4 fillets of pickled herring, halved and cut into strips, 2 beetroot cut into julienne strips, and 8 gherkins; or 125 g/¼ lb. ham cut into strips, 125 g/¼ lb. tongue cut into strips, and 8 gherkins.

'I didn't dare to make Russian salad and anyway it was impossible when you consider the preparation needed – the tiny vegetables, the mayonnaise; I would never have had the time . . . it was needed then and there. And so it came from the Restaurant Larue.'

CA, 99

Sauces

Béarnaise Sauce

	UK	US	
	1	1	shallot
	1 Tb	1 Tb	chervil
	1 Tb	1 Tb	tarragon
			salt
	6	6	black peppercorns, crushed
	4 Tb	4 Tb	dry white wine
	1 Tb	1 Tb	white wine vinegar or tarragon vinegar
120 g	4 oz.	1 stick	unsalted butter
	2	2	large egg yolks (or 3 small)
	2 drops	2 drops	lemon juice

Makes 150 ml/¼ pint/⅔ cup

Finely chop the shallot, chervil and tarragon. Put the shallot and half the chervil and tarragon in a saucepan with a little salt and the pepper, wine and vinegar. Cook over very low heat for about 20–25 minutes, until the shallot is very tender and 1 tablespoon of liquid remains. Strain and rub this mixture through a sieve into a bowl.

Cut small pieces of butter on to a plate and soften above a saucepan of simmering water, but avoid melting the butter.

Fit the bowl containing the liquid over a saucepan containing 1 inch of barely simmering water. Add the yolks, whisk for a minute, and gradually add the butter, whisking each piece in thoroughly before adding the next.

Stir with a wooden spoon until the mixture starts to thicken and coats the back of the spoon; this whole operation takes about 10 minutes altogether. Over-heating will cause the yolks to scramble and the mixture to separate, so have patience! As soon as the sauce is thick, remove it from the heat, stir in 2 drops of lemon juice and the remaining chervil and tarragon.

Taste for seasoning and pour immediately into a serving bowl. To avoid last-minute curdling it is important to remove the sauce from the hot bowl as soon as possible. Serve warm or lukewarm.

M. de Guermantes: 'Now today there was a devil of a cook who sent me up a leg of mutton with béarnaise *sauce – it was done to a turn, I must admit, but just for that very reason I took so much of it that it's still lying on my stomach.'*

VI, 384

Sauce Choron

To make this, follow the above recipe but add 1 teaspoon of tomato paste. Very good served with lamb cutlets or other grilled/broiled meats.

Mayonnaise

	UK	US	
	2	2	large egg yolks
			juice of ½ lemon
	½ tsp	½ tsp	salt
300 ml	½ pint	1¼ cups	mild olive oil*
			hot water

Beat the egg yolks in a bowl (an electric beater at the lowest speed may be used) until they start to turn a pale colour. Add salt and gradually beat in the oil, pouring in a very thin trickle to begin with, until the yolks and oil begin to emulsify. It is then possible to add the oil in a faster stream, but with caution. This mixture may curdle: if so, break another egg yolk into a clean bowl, beat for 1 minute and add the curdled mixture very slowly, thereby rebuilding the emulsion. When the mayonnaise starts to become very thick, add the lemon juice, continuing to beat until all the oil is absorbed.

Fold in a tablespoon of hot (not boiling) water, if the mayonnaise needs further thinning. Taste for seasoning, adding more lemon juice and salt if desired.

Sauce Gribiche

Similar to mayonnaise, but highly flavoured. Good with fish, boiled beef or chicken. Delicious with steamed, unpeeled potatoes (see recipe, p. 90).

	UK	US	
	2	2	large eggs
	½ tsp	½ tsp	salt
			pepper
	1 tsp	1 tsp	French mustard
230 ml	8 fl. oz.	1 cup	oil
	1 tsp	1 tsp	fresh or dried tarragon
	1 tsp	1 tsp	chopped parsley
	1 tsp	1 tsp	chopped chervil
	1 tsp	1 tsp	chopped gherkins
	1 tsp	1 tsp	chopped capers
			juice of ½ lemon
	1 tsp	1 tsp	vinegar

Boil eggs for 10 minutes, drain and cover with cold water. Shell them and chop the whites finely. Place the yolks in a small bowl; add the salt, pepper and mustard and blend well. Using an electric beater at low speed, add the oil in a fine trickle at first, until oil and yolks begin to emulsify. Then it is possible to add the oil in a faster stream, but with caution. This mixture may curdle; if it does so, break an egg yolk into a clean bowl, beat for 1 minute and add the curdled mixture slowly, thereby rebuilding the emulsion.

When all the oil has been absorbed, stir in the chopped egg whites, tarragon, parsley, chervil, gherkins, capers, lemon juice and vinegar.

* Vegetable (or sunflower or groundnut) oil may be substituted for all or part of the olive oil.

'Altogether, my aunt used to treat him [Swann] with scant ceremony. Since she was of the opinion that he ought to feel flattered by our invitations, she thought it only right and proper that he should never come to see us in summer without a basket of peaches or raspberries from his garden, and that from each of his visits to Italy he should bring back some photographs of old masters for me.

'It seemed quite natural, therefore, to send to him whenever we wanted a recipe for a gribiche sauce or for a pineapple salad for one of our big dinner-parties, to which he himself would not be invited, not seeming of sufficient importance to be served up to new friends who might be in our house for the first time.'

I, 22

Madeira Sauce

Strictly speaking, a madeira sauce needs long preparation and should include a demi-glace made from sauce espagnole and a brown stock. The following is a shortened version more suited to the ordinary household.

	UK	US	
	2	2	small carrots
	1	1	medium onion
30 g	1 oz.	¼ stick	butter
	1 Tb	1 Tb	flour
300 ml	½ pint	1¼ cups	beef stock
	2 Tb	2 Tb	tomato sauce, *or*
	1 Tb	1 Tb	tomato paste
			juice of ½ lemon
100 ml	4 fl. oz.	½ cup	madeira
			salt, pepper

Proust, on reading a letter from his former chauffeur Nicolas Cottin, who became a chef in the army, explains: '" He is lost! Instead of making madeira sauce or port sauce, he's got to drink it. Look how fat he has become."'

CA, 62

Wash and scrape the carrots and grate them coarsely. Finely chop the onions. Melt the butter in a frying pan over medium heat, add the vegetables and cook until they turn brown, turning occasionally. Sprinkle in the flour and cook until it browns; add the stock, tomato sauce or paste, and cook, covered, for half an hour. Rub through a sieve into a saucepan, stir in the lemon juice and madeira and bring to the boil. Simmer 1 minute.

Check for seasoning, adding salt and pepper if necessary.

If port is substituted for madeira, this becomes *Sauce au Porto*.

Four-handed method of straining sauces through a tammy cloth. *La Cuisine d'aujourd'hui* by Urbain Dubois, 1900.

Sauce Velouté de Poisson

To accompany brill (see recipe, p. 42), turbot or other fish. This is very similar to a Béchamel sauce except that stock (in this case fish stock) is substituted for milk. For the stock use bones and head of 4 sole, plaice/flounder or other fish.

	UK	US	
	1¾ pints	4½ cups	water
115 ml	4 fl. oz.	½ cup	dry white wine
	1	1	small onion, roughly chopped
	1	1	sprig of thyme
	2	2	sprigs of parsley
	1	1	bayleaf
30 g	1 oz.	2 Tb	butter
30 g	1 oz.	4 Tb	flour
	1 tsp	1 tsp	salt
			pepper
			grated nutmeg (2 pinches)
115 ml	4 fl. oz.	½ cup	double/heavy cream (optional)

Put the fish bones, water, wine, onion, thyme, parsley and bayleaf in a saucepan and bring to the boil. Cook, covered, for half an hour, then strain and reduce by further cooking to 450 ml/¾ pint/2 cups fish stock.

Melt the butter in a saucepan; add the flour and stir, off the heat, until well mixed. Add the fish stock and stir until thick and smooth. Add salt, pepper and nutmeg and barely cook over very low heat for 10 minutes, stirring occasionally. This will ensure that the flavour of the sauce matures and the floury taste disappears. Stir in the cream (if used) before serving.

The sauce may be prepared beforehand (in which case a little melted butter dribbled over the top will prevent a skin forming) and reheated in a bowl over simmering water. If it becomes lumpy, rub through a sieve at the last moment. It may also be enriched and thickened by beating in two egg yolks instead of the cream.

Position of the hands in mixing and stirring off the heat. From *The Royal Cookery Book* by Jules Gouffe, 1868.

Prawn Sauce · Sauce aux Crevettes

To accompany fillets of sole, brill or turbot, or quenelles.

	UK	US	
125 g	¼ lb.	¼ lb.	cooked peeled prawns/ shrimps
60 g	2 oz.	½ stick	butter
60 g	2 oz.	½ cup	flour
800 ml	28 fl. oz.	3½ cups	fish stock, made from 700 g/ 1½ lb. fish bones and skin and water to cover, boiled for 30 minutes and strained
	2 tsp	2 tsp	tomato paste
	1 Tb	1 Tb	vermouth or dry white wine
	1 tsp	1 tsp	lemon juice
			pinch of cayenne pepper
			salt, pepper
	8	8	cooked unpeeled prawns/ shrimps for decoration

Serves 8

Liquidize the prawns with half the fish stock in the blender for 15 seconds.

Melt the butter in a saucepan, add the flour and stir well, off the heat, until they are amalgamated. Pour in all the stock and liquidized prawns and stir until smooth. Add the tomato paste, vermouth or wine, lemon juice, cayenne, salt and pepper to taste, and simmer for 7 minutes, stirring occasionally. Rub through a sieve and, when the fish or quenelles are ready, heat the sauce and pour it over them, garnishing with the remaining (unpeeled) prawns/shrimps.

Cream Sauce

To accompany brill or other fish.

	UK	US	
	4	4	sole or plaice/flounder (bones and heads only)
	4 Tb	4 Tb	dry vermouth
			salt
230 ml	8 fl. oz.	1 cup	double/heavy cream

Cover the fishbones with water, add dry vermouth and simmer for 1 hour. Strain through cheesecloth and cook for another ½ hour until reduced to approximately 230 ml/8 fl. oz./1 cup of fish stock. Add salt and cream and barely simmer over very low heat for 1 hour or, better still, over the pilot light for 4 hours, until the sauce is further reduced and thickened. Long and slow cooking of all stages of this sauce is recommended, to achieve perfection of flavour and a velvet texture.

Sauce Hollandaise

	UK	US	
	4	4	egg yolks
			pinch of salt
225 g	8 oz.	2 sticks	unsalted/sweet butter
	1 tsp	1 tsp	lemon juice

Makes about 400 ml/14 fl. oz./1¾ cups

Break the egg yolks into a heatproof bowl and add the salt. Beat until thick and lemon-coloured. Cut the butter into small slices, put them on a heatproof plate and allow to soften over a pan of hot water.

Fit the bowl of egg yolks over a pan of simmering (not boiling) water and add the butter piece by piece, stirring briskly and constantly with a wooden spoon. Continue cooking and stirring until the sauce thickens and coats the back of the spoon. Add the lemon juice and taste for additional seasoning. Remove from the heat and immediately pour into a serving jug to stop further cooking and prevent curdling.

Should the sauce curdle, start again with a clean bowl and another egg yolk. Beat the yolk and gradually add the curdled mixture, thereby rebuilding the emulsion.

Mousseline Sauce

	UK	US	
400 ml	14 fl. oz.	1¾ cups	hollandaise sauce (recipe as above)
100 ml	4 fl. oz.	½ cup	double/heavy cream

Prepare the hollandaise sauce. Shortly before serving, whip the cream until floppy and fold it in.

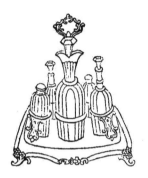

Vinaigrette Sauce

	UK	US	
230 ml	8 fl. oz.	1 cup	oil
60 ml	2 fl. oz.	¼ cup	wine vinegar
			juice of ½ lemon
	½ tsp	½ tsp	French mustard
	½ tsp	½ tsp	salt
	¼ tsp	¼ tsp	fresh ground black pepper

Combine ingredients and beat vigorously with a fork until they are well blended and form a thick emulsion.

If served with asparagus (recipe, p. 85), pour over warm asparagus but serve cold.

Clarified/Drawn Butter

	UK	US	
125 g	4 oz.	1 stick	unsalted/sweet butter
			pinch of salt

Melt the butter over very low heat. As soon as it is liquid, remove from the heat and leave to cool but not harden. Strain out the sediment through a fine sieve lined with cheesecloth. Stir in the salt and serve.

This butter is clear and shiny, and looks better than ordinary melted butter. It is also good for frying because it is free of sediment and therefore less likely to burn.

Lemon Butter

	UK	US	
125 g	4 oz.	1 stick	unsalted/sweet butter
			pinch of salt
			juice of ½ lemon

Melt and strain the butter as directed in the recipe above, and stir in lemon juice to taste.

Breads

Rye Cakes · Petits Pains de Seigle

	UK	US	
30 g	1 oz.	1½ Tb	fresh yeast (or half the quantity of dried yeast)
	1 tsp	1 tsp	brown sugar
50 ml	1½ fl. oz.	3 Tb	warm water
175 g	6 oz.	1½ cups	plain white flour
175 g	6 oz.	1½ cups	rye flour
115 ml	4 fl. oz.	½ cup	milk
75 ml	3 fl. oz.	⅓ cup	water
30 g	1 oz.	2 Tb	butter
	1 tsp	1 tsp	salt
	2 tsp	2 tsp	caraway seeds
30 g	1 oz.	2 Tb	melted butter, for brushing over the rolls
			sprinkle of rock salt

Makes 18 little rolls

'It was the time of day at which the beach is crowded by itinerant and clamorous vendors, hawking cakes and sweets and biscuits. Not knowing quite what to do to shew her affection for us, the Princess [de Luxembourg] hailed the next that came by; he had nothing left but one rye-cake, of the kind one throws to the ducks. The Princess took it and said to me: "For your grandmother." '

III, 390

Dissolve the yeast with the sugar in the warm water for 15–20 minutes. Sift the flours together into a bowl. Heat the milk and the water with the butter, until the butter just melts. Make a well in the centre of the flours, add the yeast mixture and warm milk mixture and stir with a large wooden spoon or fork until thoroughly blended; add salt. Sprinkle a board or counter with some white flour and pour the dough on to it. With floury hands knead the dough for 5 minutes, adding more flour as needed, to obtain a smooth elastic dough. Lightly oil a clean bowl, put the dough in it, cover with a teacloth and put to rise in a warm place, either in the airing/linen cupboard or over a bowl of warm water, or on top of a slow oven, for an hour, until doubled in bulk.

Knead again, adding more flour only if necessary, and replace in the bowl for another hour in a warm place.

Set the oven to gas mark 4, 350° F. Punch the dough down again and work in the caraway seeds. Form into little balls, place on a baking sheet, brush over with melted butter and sprinkle with rock salt. Bake for 45 minutes.

Holy Bread · Pain Bénit

It was customary for parishioners to make for the local church a bread similar to a brioche, which was then consecrated and distributed. This bread is delicious served warm with a meal, or at the end of a meal with a hard cheese such as Cantal or Cheddar.

	UK	US	
30 g	1 oz.	1½ Tb	fresh yeast *or*
		1 heaped	
20 g	⅔ oz.	Tb	dried yeast
60 ml	2 fl. oz.	4 Tb	warm water
1 kg	2 lb. 3 oz.	8 cups	flour
450 g	1 lb	4 sticks	unsalted butter
570 ml	1 pint	2½ cups	milk
	1½ tsp	1½ tsp	salt

'But – and this more than ever from the day on which fine weather definitely set in at Combray – the proud hour of noon, descending from the steeple of Saint-Hilaire which it blazoned for a moment with the twelve points of its sonorous crown, would long have echoed about our table, beside the "holy bread", which too had come in, after church, in its familiar way; and we would still be found seated in front of our Arabian Nights plates, weighed down by the heat of the day, and even more by our heavy meal.'

I, 93

Bring the milk to the boil, then let it cool to lukewarm. Dissolve the yeast in warm water for 15 minutes until frothy. Measure out half the flour and salt and sift into a large bowl. Make a well in the centre, pour in the yeast and warm milk and stir with a fork, gradually incorporating all the flour. Stir until thoroughly mixed, cover with a teacloth and leave to rise in a warm place such as the airing/linen cupboard, or over a bowl of hot water, or on top of a low oven, for 1 hour.

Soften the butter and mix it into the dough with a fork. When thoroughly mixed, sieve in the rest of the flour and salt. Turn out on to a counter or board. Mix and work the dough with your hands, stretching and kneading it. This dough remains sticky and rough, unlike bread dough.

Butter and fill two round bread pans or charlotte moulds (1½ litres/2¼ pints/6 cups capacity) two-thirds full and leave in a warm place until the dough is well risen. Set the oven to gas mark 6, 400° F. Brush each brioche with melted butter and cook for 1 hour or until the bottom of the pan sounds hollow when you knock it. Cool on a cake rack and unmould as soon as cool enough to handle.

The church tower at Illiers-Combray. Mante-Proust Collection.

Croissants

Croissants are such a delight to cook and serve warm first thing in the morning, or with any meal, that it is advisable to make the dough the night before (2 hours) and let the dough 'rest' all night in the refrigerator. The procedure for making these croissants takes about 3½ hours, if the dough does not need to 'rest' or harden up in the refrigerator between turns.

Either bake all the croissants at one time and freeze those not consumed, or cut the dough into quarters (2 croissants can be formed from each quarter) and bake as needed. The dough will keep in the refrigerator for 2 days.

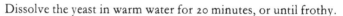

	UK	US	
15 g	½ oz.	1 Tb	fresh yeast, *or*
10 g	⅓ oz.	½ Tb	dried yeast
60 ml	2 fl. oz.	¼ cup	warm water
250 g	9 oz.	2 cups	flour
	1 tsp.	1 tsp	salt
115 ml	4 fl. oz.	½ cup	milk
150 g	5 oz.	1¼ sticks	unsalted butter
	1	1	egg yolk, beaten, for glazing

Makes 8 large croissants

Dissolve the yeast in warm water for 20 minutes, or until frothy.

Heat the milk to lukewarm.

Sift the flour with the salt into a large bowl. Make a well in the flour and pour in the milk and the yeast mixture; stir with a wooden fork or spoon, gradually incorporating the flour until it becomes a rough dough. Turn on to a floured board or counter and with floured hands knead for 5 minutes or until it becomes a smooth, elastic dough. Lightly oil a clean bowl, put the dough into it, cover with a clean cloth, and put to rise in a warm place, either in the airing/linen cupboard or over a bowl of hot water or on top of a low oven, for about an hour or until it doubles in bulk.

Flour the counter again and punch down the dough. Knead for 2 minutes, then form it into a small rectangle. Lightly roll the dough with a rolling pin into a rectangle 15 in. long, 5 in. wide and ⅜ in. thick, with the length of the rectangle stretching away from you.

Squeeze the butter in a bowl of cold water with your hands, or work it with a knife until it is soft and pliable. It should have the same consistency as the dough. Spread half the butter on the two-thirds of the dough furthest away from you. Now bring up the first third (nearest to you) over the middle third and fold the last third on top. Press down gently with your hands and turn the dough once so that the side edges are facing you. Close the edges with a little pressure from the rolling pin, to prevent the butter squeezing out. Roll out to the same-sized rectangle again and spread the rest of the butter as before. Fold again, turn and close the edges again.

You have now rolled and turned twice, adding butter both times. Repeat the process 4 more times, without the addition of butter (see note below). Place in greaseproof paper or in a plastic bag and let it rest in the refrigerator for 1 hour, or overnight.

Set the oven to gas mark 7, 425° F. Roll out the dough to a large sheet, approximately 12 in. square and ¼ in. thick. Cut this into 4 pieces about 6 in. square, and cut each of these diagonally to make 8 triangles. Roll up the triangles from the longest side to the furthest point and fasten with a little water. Curve them into crescent shapes and place them on a baking sheet which has been previously brushed with water. Leave for 15 minutes at room temperature, until they have risen a little. Brush the beaten egg yolk mixed with a tablespoon of water and bake for 20 minutes if you are going to serve them right away, or 15 minutes if they are to be frozen and re-heated later.

Note. To make this dough successfully, the butter needs to be just soft enough to spread, so avoid letting it become warm or melted, as this will make it more likely to break through the dough.

Always roll lightly and firmly, sprinkling more flour on the counter and on the rolling pin as it is needed, especially if the butter breaks through the dough. Use as little extra flour as possible, to ensure a light dough.

Given some extra flour and a cool day, it is possible to roll out and fold 6 times without the dough having to 'rest'. If it is a hot day and the butter is breaking through, the dough can be put to 'rest' in the refrigerator for 20 minutes between the turns.

Marcel makes the acquaintance of two maids who are accompanying an old foreign lady at the hotel in Balbec. One is Marie Gineste and the other Céleste Albaret. 'They often came in the morning to see me when I was still in bed. . . . while I dipped crescent rolls in my milk, Céleste would say to me: "Oh! Little black devil with hair of jet, O profound wickedness! I don't know what your mother was thinking of when she made you, for you are just like a bird. . . . Look at him throwing away his crescent because it touched the bed." '

VII, 342–3

Proust in childhood. Collection C. Albaret.

Bread Rolls · Boules, Petits Pains

	UK	US	
30 g	1 oz.	1½ Tb	fresh yeast, *or*
		1 Tb	
20 g	⅔ oz.	heaped	dried yeast
60 ml	2 fl. oz.	¼ cup	warm water
1 kg	2 lb. 3 oz.	8 cups	flour
	2 tsp	2 tsp	salt
115 g	4 oz.	1 stick	butter
300 ml	½ pint	1¼ cups	milk
150 ml	¼ pint	⅔ cup	water
	1	1	egg, beaten, for glazing
			rock salt

Makes approximately 16 rolls

Dissolve the yeast in the warm water for 15 minutes.

Sift the flour and salt into a large bowl. Heat the milk with the water and butter until they are warm and the butter is melted. Make a well in the centre of the flour and pour in the yeast and warm milk and butter. Stir with a fork, gradually incorporating all the flour. Pour this rough dough on to a board or counter and knead for 7–10 minutes until it is smooth and elastic. Put the dough in a clean, lightly oiled bowl, cover with a teacloth and put to rise in a warm place, either in the airing/linen cupboard, over another bowl of hot water or on top of a low oven, for 45 minutes.

Knock down the dough: that is, put it on a board or counter and knead again for 5 minutes. Shape into a long roll and cut off small pieces to shape into balls and place on a baking sheet.

Set the oven to gas mark 8, 450° F., and let the rolls rise on top of the oven for 20 minutes. Brush the rolls with beaten egg, cut a cross on the top of each one, sprinkle with rock salt and bake for 7 minutes, then turn the oven down to gas mark 6, 400° F., and cook another 15 minutes. Serve warm.

Cakes and Pastries

Chocolate Cake · Gâteau au Chocolat

The finished cake entails the preparation of the cake layers (2 large and 2 small), chocolate slabs for decoration, the filling and the icing/frosting. It is recommended that the slabs are prepared first, then the cake, the filling and the icing/frosting.

	UK	US	
	9	9	large eggs
230 g	8 oz.	1 cup	caster/fine sugar
700 g	1 lb. 8 oz.	24 squares	Menier, Bournville or Baker's semi-sweet chocolate
500 g	1 lb. 1½ oz.	4 sticks + 1 Tb	unsalted butter

cake:

	UK	US	
	7	7	large eggs
230 g	8 oz.	1 cup	caster/fine sugar
300 g	10 oz.	10 squares	Menier, Bournville or Baker's semi-sweet chocolate
300 g	10 oz.	2½ sticks	unsalted butter at room temperature
	1 tsp	1 tsp	vanilla essence
75 ml	3 fl. oz.	⅓ cup	milk
150 g	5 oz.	1 cup + 1 Tb	flour
	½ tsp	½ tsp	salt
75 g	3 oz.	¾ cup	ground almonds

slabs:

	UK	US	
120 g	4 oz.	4 squares	plain or semi-sweet chocolate as above

filling:

	UK	US	
	2	2	egg yolks
150 g	5 oz.	1¼ sticks	unsalted butter, softened
	½ tsp	½ tsp	vanilla essence
90 g	3 oz.	3 squares	plain or semi-sweet chocolate as above

icing/frosting:

	UK	US	
200 g	7 oz.	7 squares	plain or semi-sweet chocolate as above
50 g	1½ oz.	3 Tb	unsalted butter
	12	12	glacé cherries

'On those tea-party days . . . I felt that I could already behold the majesty of the chocolate cake, encircled by plates heaped with little cakes, and by tiny napkins of grey damask with figures on them. . . . And she [Gilberte] would make us go into the dining-room, as sombre as the interior of an Asiatic Temple painted by Rembrandt, in which an architectural cake, as gracious and sociable as it was imposing, seemed to be enthroned there in any event, in case the fancy seized Gilberte to discrown it of its chocolate battlements and to hew down the steep brown slopes of its ramparts, baked in the oven like the bastions of the palace of Darius. Better still, in proceeding to the demolition of that Babylonitish pastry, Gilberte did not consider only her own hunger; she inquired also after mine, while she extracted for me from the crumbling monument a whole glazed slab jewelled with scarlet fruits, in the oriental style.'

III, 110

Slabs

Melt the chocolate over simmering water and as soon as it is soft spread it with a spatula on to a piece of greaseproof paper over an area approximately 8½ in. square and about ⅛ in. thick. When the chocolate has hardened somewhat, cut into little slabs 1½ in. square and leave until required for the final decoration of the cake, when all you need to do is peel them off the paper. Makes approximately 25.

Cake

Set the oven to gas mark 4, 350° F. Butter and flour two cake tins, 10 in. and 8 in. in diameter respectively. Weigh out the sugar, flour, butter and ground almonds. Sieve together the flour and salt. Break up the chocolate and put to melt in a bowl over simmering water. Beat the eggs, using an electric beater if desired, until very foamy and three times their original volume; then gradually add the sugar. Stop beating and stir the butter into the melted chocolate. It is a good idea not to let the chocolate get too hot as it may become lumpy; take it off the heat as soon as it softens and, still off the heat, add the butter, stirring until it melts. Slowly pour this into the egg and sugar mixture, beating continuously, then add the vanilla and milk. With a rubber spatula fold in the flour and ground almonds very carefully, slowly and thoroughly, using a 'figure of eight' movement, so as not to lose the airiness of the mixture. Pour into the cake pans and cook for one hour or until the edges of the cakes leave the sides of their pans. Stand each on a cake rack and when lukewarm unmould and cool thoroughly before final assembly.

Filling

While the cake is baking, put the chocolate to melt as above. Put 2 egg yolks into a small bowl, add the softened butter and the vanilla and then beat until light and creamy. When the chocolate has melted, add this to the mixture, beating until all is smooth. Put in the refrigerator to chill.

Icing/frosting (prepare this when the cake is ready to be assembled)

Melt the chocolate in a bowl over simmering water; when soft, remove from the heat and stir in the butter.

To assemble the cake, trim any crumbly parts from the cakes, and divide each into two layers. When handling these thin layers, slide the bottom of a cake pan or a flat metal sheet under them to prevent breakage. Put the *icing* chocolate on to melt. Lay one of the larger layers on a platter and cover it with a third of the *filling*; top with the next layer and spread another third of the *filling* over this layer, but not to the edges: cover only an area in the centre 8 in. in diameter so that the smaller layers will cover it. Now put one of the smaller layers on, cover with the rest of the *filling* and top with the final layer. Chop 6 glacé cherries and put on the top of the cake.

Ice the cake with a knife or spatula. Start at the top, partially covering the cherries, and work down, sticking the slabs upright round the edge of each layer as you ice it, and finally sticking pieces of glacé cherry on to a few of the slabs using some of the icing chocolate. Save one slab for the centre of the cake. The spreading of the icing can be as smooth or as rough as you like.

If you possess two square cake tins 8 in. and 10 in. square, you might utilize these, and your cake will more closely resemble a Babylonian ziggurat.

Almond Cake · Gâteau d'Amandes

	UK	US	
	3	3	eggs
	½ tsp	½ tsp	salt
150 g	5 oz.	⅔ cup	caster/fine sugar
		1 cup	
150 g	5 oz.	+ 1 Tb	flour
	2 Tb	2 Tb	milk
120 g	4 oz.	1 stick	butter, melted
120 g	4 oz.	1 cup	toasted slivered almonds
			grated rind of ½ lemon
			icing/confectioners' sugar

To toast the slivered almonds, put them in a frying pan over medium heat. Once they begin to colour, turn them frequently so that they toast evenly. Alternatively, lay them in a roasting pan and bake 7 minutes in the oven at gas mark 4, 350° F.

Butter and flour an 8-in. cake tin. Heat the oven to gas mark 5, 375° F.

Beat the eggs and the salt together, using an electric beater if desired, for 5 minutes until the mixture is very thick and pale yellow. Gradually add the sugar, then the flour, previously sifted, the milk and finally the melted butter. Stir in the lemon rind and the almonds, saving a few for decoration.

Bake for 35–40 minutes or until the cake leaves the side of the pan. Stand on a cake rack for 10 minutes before removing from cake pan. When cool, dust with a little icing/confectioner's sugar and sprinkle with a few almonds.

'When, before turning to leave the church, I made a genuflection before the altar, I felt suddenly, as I rose again, a bitter-sweet fragrance of almond steal towards me from the hawthorn-blossom, and then I noticed that on the flowers themselves were little spots of a creamier colour, in which I imagined that this fragrance must lie concealed, as the taste of an almond cake lay in the burned parts, or the sweetness of Mlle Vinteuil's cheeks beneath their freckles. Despite the heavy, motionless silence of the hawthorns, these gusts of fragrance came to me like the murmuring of an intense vitality, with which the whole altar was quivering like a roadside hedge explored by living antennae.'

I, 153

'Diplomatic' Cakes · Diplomates

	UK	US	
45 g	1½ oz.	2 Tb	mixed currants and glacé fruits
	2 Tb	2 Tb	rum
		½ stick	
70 g	2½ oz.	+ 1 Tb	butter
45 g	1½ oz.	3 Tb	caster/fine sugar
		3 heaped	
45 g	1½ oz.	Tb	ground almonds
	1 Tb	1 Tb	potato or rice flour
	1	1	egg, beaten
	1 Tb	1 Tb	apricot jam
			fondant icing flavoured with rum (see petits fours recipe, p. 124)

'No sooner did they sit down at the table covered with a cloth embroidered in red, beneath the painted panels, to partake of the rock cakes, Norman puff pastry, tartlets shaped like boats filled with cherries like beads of coral, "diplomatic" cakes, than these guests were subjected, by the proximity of the great bowl of azure upon which the window opened, and which you could not help seeing when you looked at them, to a profound alteration, a transmutation which changed them into something more precious than before.'

VIII, 202

Soak currants and fruit in rum for half an hour.

Cream the butter, using an electric beater if desired. When light and fluffy, add the sugar, ground almonds, potato flour and egg. Beat well and stir in the fruits and rum.

Set the oven to gas mark 6, 400° F. Butter and flour 6 small oval, brioche or barquette moulds. Spoon in the mixture and bake for 15–17 minutes, until the edges of the cakes begin to come away from the sides of the moulds.

Invert the cakes on to a cake rack and let them cool. Melt the apricot jam and brush on a thin layer. Thin down the fondant with a tablespoon of rum and sugar syrup and pour over cakes.

Spiced Cake · Pain d'Epice

	UK	US	
350 g	12 oz.	2¾ cups	rye flour
450 g	1 lb.	1½ cups	honey
120 g	4 oz.	⅔ cup	brown sugar
			pinch of salt
	1½ tsp	1½ tsp	baking powder
	½ tsp	½ tsp	anise seeds
			grated rind of ½ lemon
			grated rind of ½ orange
	½ tsp	½ tsp	nutmeg
	½ tsp	½ tsp	ground allspice
115 ml	4 fl. oz.	½ cup	boiling water

Serves 10

Set the oven to gas mark 4, 350° F.

Sift the flour, salt and baking powder together into a bowl. Add the rest of the ingredients and beat hard with a wooden spoon. Butter a 10 in. × 5½ in. × 3 in. loaf tin, fill with the mixture and bake for 1 hour 10 minutes.

Cool to lukewarm and invert on to a cake rack to cool completely. This cake keeps well for 2–3 weeks if wrapped, or stored in an airtight box.

'Tell me what you eat, and I will tell you what you are' – Brillat-Savarin. From *L'Art de bien manger* by E. Richardin, 1910.

'*One day we had gone with Gilberte to the stall of our own special vendor, who was always particularly nice to us, since it was to her that M. Swann used to send for his* pain d'épice, *of which, for reasons of health, (he suffered from a racial eczema, and from the constipation of the prophets) he consumed a great quantity . . .*'

II, 254

Gâteau St Honoré

This is made up of a sweet pastry base surrounded with a choux paste circle, topped with about 10 cream-filled profiteroles coated with caramel and filled with Saint-Honoré cream. The whole cake may be decorated with whipped cream and spun sugar.

sweet pastry:

	UK	US	
230 g	8 oz.	1¾ cups	flour
30 g	1 oz.	¼ cup	icing/confectioners' sugar
	½ tsp	½ tsp	salt
150 g	5 oz.	1¼ sticks	butter
	2	2	egg yolks
	2 Tb	2 Tb	water

choux paste:

See éclair recipe, p. 117, plus

	UK	US	
150 ml	¼ pint	⅔ cup	double/heavy cream

caramel:

	UK	US	
150 g	5 oz.	⅔ cup	sugar
115 ml	4 fl. oz.	½ cup	water

Saint-Honoré cream:

	UK	US	
	4	4	eggs, separated
90 g	3 oz.	¾ cup	icing/confectioners' sugar
30 g	1 oz.	2 Tb	flour
			pinch of salt
300 ml	½ pint	1¼ cups	milk
	1 tsp	1 tsp	vanilla essence
			juice of ½ lemon (optional)
			grated rind of 1 orange (optional)
			grated rind of ½ lemon (optional)
	1 tsp	1 tsp	chopped glacé fruits (optional)

Serves 8

'Just as we reached the house my mother discovered that we had forgotten the "Saint-Honoré", and asked my father to go back with me and tell them to send it up at once.'

I, 170

Make pastry by sifting the flour, sugar and salt together into a large bowl. Cut the butter into pieces and rub it into the flour with the fingertips. Then change to rubbing the pastry between the fingers of both hands until the mixture resembles fine crumbs. Mix the yolks with 2 tablespoons of water, beating with a fork. Make a well in the flour and butter mixture, add the yolks and water and gradually incorporate the two with a fork until the pastry sticks together in one mass. Knead lightly with the hands until a smooth pastry is attained. Deft and quick handling helps to ensure a light pastry.

Roll out to a 10-in. circle on a floured surface. Roll the pastry round the rolling pin and unroll on to greaseproof paper laid on a baking sheet. Prick all over with a fork. Refrigerate while preparing the choux paste.

When the choux paste is ready, set the oven to gas mark 8, 450° F. Take the sweet pastry base out of the refrigerator and make a circular indentation with your finger all round the top of the pastry circle just $\frac{1}{2}$ in. away from the edge. Spoon some choux paste into a pastry bag with a $\frac{1}{2}$-in. nozzle and pipe a thick border round the edge of the top of the pastry circle, into the indentation you have made. Make sure it is a thick border by slowly pushing as much paste as possible through the nozzle as you move round the circle. This is to ensure a well-puffed-up border for the gâteau.

Put in the oven for 10 minutes at gas mark 8, 450° F., and then turn down to gas mark 6, 400° F., for the next 15–20 minutes, after which the border should be well puffed up and the pastry circle light brown. Remove from the oven and make small holes in the choux paste with the tip of a sharp knife or skewer to let the steam escape. Put back into the bottom of the oven for 10 minutes to dry out further.

Reset the oven to gas mark 8, 450° F. Make miniature balls of choux paste (profiteroles), 1 in. in diameter, by squeezing the remaining paste through the $\frac{1}{2}$-in. nozzle on to a baking sheet. (Make extra profiteroles or éclairs with any remaining paste.) Cook for 15 minutes, remove, and prick holes in them with a sharp knife or skewer to release the steam. Turn off the oven and put the profiteroles back for 15 minutes to dry out further.

Make the caramel by boiling the water and sugar together until thick and caramel-coloured. Dip the choux balls (profiteroles) in the caramel, holding them with tongs, and stick them on the border of the cake base, leaving the holes exposed so that they can be filled with whipped cream later. Pour or spoon caramel on top of the profiteroles as well.

To make Saint-Honoré cream, separate the eggs into two different bowls, reserving the whites for later. Heat the milk in a saucepan over medium heat not quite to boiling point. Sift the sugar with the flour and salt. Beat the egg yolks, using an electric beater if desired; gradually add the sugar and flour and finally the hot milk, lowering the speed of the beater as you do this. Scrape the sides with a spatula, return this mixture to the saucepan and stir constantly with a wooden spoon over low heat until the mixture thickens and coats the back of the spoon. Stir in the vanilla essence and lemon juice (if using), then sieve into a bowl and put to cool. Add the orange and lemon rind (if using) and whisk occasionally to prevent a skin forming.

When the 'cream' is cool, whip the egg whites until they are stiff and fold them in with a rubber spatula.

Whip the double/heavy cream until stiff and fill the profiteroles, using an $\frac{1}{8}$-in. nozzle on a pastry bag. Spoon the Saint-Honoré cream on to the pastry base, sprinkle with glacé fruits and decorate with rosettes of whipped cream and spun sugar if desired.

Shortbread · Galette Normande

	UK	US	
350 g	12 oz.	3 cups	flour
			pinch of salt
230 g	8 oz.	2 sticks	butter, diced
100 g	3½ oz.	½ cup	vanilla sugar
	2	2	eggs
60 ml	2 fl. oz.	⅓ cup	double/heavy cream
			butter, for baking trays
			icing/confectioners' sugar, to decorate

Makes 1 large shortbread and 1 dozen shortbread biscuits/cookies

'I had difficulty in recognizing the melting, savoury morsel which I had beside me the other afternoon at teatime, on the terrace at Balbec, in the galette normande *that I now saw, hard as a rock, in which the faithful would in vain have tried to set their teeth.'*

VIII, 84

Sift the flour and salt into a bowl. Rub in the butter with your fingertips, then rub lightly between the palms of the hands until a crumbly mixture is obtained. Stir in the sugar.

Beat together 1 whole egg and 1 egg yolk, reserving the remaining white for glazing the shortbread. Add beaten eggs and cream to the flour mixture and mix well with a fork. Then gather it together into a ball and knead briefly until smooth. Roll it into a ball again, put it into a plastic bag and chill it in the refrigerator for 45 minutes.

On a floured surface, roll the dough out into a long rectangle stretching away from you. Fold in three, turn a folded edge towards you and roll out into a rectangle again. Repeat this procedure three more times, using a little more flour if necessary.

Preheat the oven to gas mark 6, 400° F. Divide the dough into two pieces and roll one piece into a round 10 in. in diameter. Place this on a buttered baking tray. With two small, sharp knives held together in one hand, make three or four crosswise incisions in the surface of the shortbread, then three or four in the opposite direction to make diamond shapes.

Beat the reserved egg white with a fork until foamy and brush it over the surface of the shortbread. Bake for 25 minutes, or until the shortbread is golden brown. Allow to cool slightly on the baking tray before transferring to a wire rack; leave until quite cold.

Meanwhile, roll out the remaining dough about ½ in. thick and cut into small rounds with a pastry cutter. Arrange them on (the same) buttered baking tray with a spatula and bake for 10 minutes.

Transfer to a wire cooling rack and while still warm dust with sifted icing/confectioners' sugar.

Coffee Eclair · Eclair au Café

choux paste:

	UK	US	
300 ml	½ pint	1¼ cups	water
120 g	4 oz.	1 stick	butter, cut in pieces
145 g	5 oz.	1¼ cups	flour
			pinch of salt
	4	4	small eggs *or*
	3½	3½	large eggs

icing:

	UK	US	
60 g	2 oz.	½ cup	icing/confectioners' sugar
	1 Tb	1 Tb	strong coffee

or use fondant icing, see recipe, p. 125.

filling:

	UK	US	
300 ml	½ pint	1¼ cups	double/heavy cream
	1	1	egg white
	1 Tb	1 Tb	strong coffee, sweetened with 1 Tb icing/confectioners' sugar

Makes 12

'*When Elstir asked me to come with him so that he might introduce me to Albertine, who was sitting a little farther down the room, I first of all finished eating a coffee* éclair *and, with a show of keen interest, asked an old gentleman whose acquaintance I had just made (and thought that I might, perhaps, offer him the rose in my buttonhole which he had admired) to tell me more about the old Norman fairs.*'

IV, 238

Set the oven to gas mark 8, 450° F. Sieve the flour with the salt. Heat the water and butter together in a saucepan until the water is boiling and the butter melted. Add the flour all at once and stir with a wooden spoon until the mixture is amalgamated and leaves the side of the saucepan. Take off the heat and put into a bowl. Beat in the eggs one at a time with the dough hooks of an electric beater or with a wooden spoon. It is important to beat long and hard, incorporating each egg completely before adding the next one. The paste should eventually be shiny and smooth, and over-beating will only improve its quality.

Put in a pastry bag with a ½-in. nozzle and push thick 3-in. lengths on to a baking sheet. Bake for 20 minutes, take out and make a slit along the side of each éclair for the steam to escape. Turn off the oven and put the éclairs back in, to dry out thoroughly, for another 15 minutes.*

Make the icing by mixing the coffee with the icing/confectioners' sugar until smooth. Coat the tops of the éclairs.

Whip the double/heavy cream with the sweetened coffee until stiff. Beat the egg white until stiff and fold into the cream. Fill the éclairs with this mixture just before serving.

---

* Choux paste can also be made into profiteroles (choux balls) by squeezing out very small balls, about 1 in. in diameter, on to a baking sheet. Bake for 15 minutes, prick a hole in each with the point of a sharp knife or skewer to let the steam out, and dry as directed for éclairs.

Both empty éclairs and profiteroles freeze well, but might need to be re-heated in a hot oven to regain their crispness before serving.

Buckwheat Pancakes · Crêpes de Blé Noir

From *Les Bons Plats de France – Les Plats Nationaux* by 'Pampille' (Mme Léon Daudet), 1919:

To be successful with these buckwheat crêpes, one has to have a Breton chimney, a Breton fire, a Breton *galettière* (the *galettière* is a flat frying pan without an edge, and with a small handle), a Breton wooden spatula, a Breton scraper (*raclette*), a Breton cook, Breton wheat and a Breton soul. When all these requirements have been met, one can start to make these crêpes: mix equal quantities of water, buckwheat flour and milk and whisk well until a smooth and liquid batter is obtained; keep in a clean bowl.

Put the *galettière* on a rush fire, melt a sliver of fat on the *galettière* and spread it all over, then put on a knob of butter and let it melt and sizzle; then pour a soup ladle of batter on to the *galettière*: the crêpe must be made in three movements.

1 With the scraper spread the batter all over the surface of the *galettière*.
2 With the wooden spatula, turn the crêpes as they brown.
3 As they cook, take them quickly off the heat, put them on a wooden tray and make 200 or 300 crêpes, piling them one on top of the other.

This crêpe is excellent hot with sugar, or with sour milk.

It is even better with an egg broken inside, then folded in four like a handkerchief. And it is also excellent reheated on the *galettière* with a little butter.

One must drink a pitcher of cider with these Breton crêpes.

All over France, a version of these lovely Breton crêpes with a large variety of fillings can be bought from street stalls. As it is impossible to obtain all the prerequisites of the recipe by Pampille outside Brittany, the following is a recipe for a much smaller amount of small crêpes which can be made in an ordinary household. They have an intriguing taste which is both slightly sour and nutty. Spread with sour cream or *rillettes* (see recipe, p. 24), or serve with grilled sausages or slices of bacon.

	UK	US	
180 g	6 oz.	1 cup	buckwheat flour
150 ml	¼ pt	⅔ cup	water
150 ml	¼ pt	⅔ cup	milk
	½ tsp	½ tsp	salt
30 g	1 oz.	¼ stick	melted butter
			extra butter to fry with

Makes 5 large (7-in.) or 10 small (4½-in.) pancakes

Whisk all the ingredients together and let stand for half an hour. Heat a heavy frying pan over medium heat and melt some butter in it: when it sizzles pour in some batter and tip the pan all round so that the batter covers the bottom of the pan in a thin layer. Cook until the edges are crisp and brown, then turn and brown the other side. Proceed with the rest of the batter, adding more butter to the pan as needed. Serve as soon as they are made or keep warm in a very low oven. These crêpes will freeze well, but should be reheated briefly in a hot oven before serving.

Rum Babas · Babas au Rhum

	UK	US	
30 g	1 oz.	1½ Tb	fresh yeast *or*
20 g	⅔ oz.	1 Tb	dried yeast
60 ml	2 fl. oz.	4 Tb	lukewarm water
115 ml	4 fl. oz.	½ cup	milk
	3	3	large eggs
350 g	12 oz.	2¾ cups	flour
120 g	4 oz.	1 stick	unsalted butter
	½ tsp	½ tsp	salt
	1 Tb	1 Tb	sugar
			grated rind of lemon
120 g	4 oz.	⅔ cup	currants

syrup and garnish:

430 ml	¾ pint	2 cups	water
450 g	1 lb.	2 cups	sugar
	1 Tb	1 Tb	glucose or corn syrup
115 g	4 fl. oz.	½ cup	dark rum
300 ml	½ pint	1¼ cups	double/heavy cream

Makes 6 small babas and 1 large baba au rhum *serving 12 people*

'No babas?' 'Sorry, madam, but an English lady has just eaten the last two dozen.'

'Other vendors came up; she [the Princesse de Luxembourg] stuffed my pockets with everything that they had, tied up in packets, comfits, sponge-cakes, sugar-sticks. "You will eat some yourself," she told me, "and give some to your grandmother," and she had the vendors paid by the little negro page, dressed in red satin, who followed her everywhere and was a nine days' wonder upon the beach.'

III, 390

Dissolve the yeast in lukewarm water for 15 minutes. Heat the milk to lukewarm.

Sieve the flour into a large bowl, make a well in it and break in the eggs. Add the milk and yeast and stir all together with a wooden fork or spoon until the mixture is blended. Continue to beat for 10 minutes, using the dough hooks of an electric beater if available, until the mixture is quite smooth.

Cover the bowl with a teacloth and leave to rise in a warm place, either in the airing/linen cupboard, over a bowl of hot water or on top of a low oven, for 45 minutes or until it doubles in bulk.

In the meantime soften the butter by cutting it into small pieces on a plate and putting the plate on top of a saucepan of boiling water for a minute or two. When the dough has risen stir in the butter, sugar, currants, salt and lemon rind. Beat for 2 minutes.

Butter and lightly flour 6 small baba or brioche moulds and a savarin mould (1·75 litre/3 pint/7½ cup size). Fill them one-third full with the dough and let it rise again on top of the oven for 20–30 minutes. Ten minutes before the end of this time, set the oven to gas mark 6, 400° F.

Make the syrup by boiling together the water, sugar and glucose for 20 minutes. Add the rum when the syrup is tepid.

Bake the savarin mould for 25 minutes in the middle of the oven with the small baba moulds on a baking sheet underneath. Take the small babas out after 15 minutes. Allow to cool briefly, then loosen and unmould on to a dish. Prick the babas all over with a toothpick and pour over the syrup, basting from time to time until the syrup has soaked in.

Whip the cream until stiff and garnish the inside of the large baba with it.

'One day in winter, as I came home, my mother, seeing that I was cold, offered me some tea, a thing I did not ordinarily take. I declined at first, and then, for no particular reason, changed my mind. She sent out for one of those short, plump little cakes, called "petites madeleines", which look as though they had been moulded in the fluted scallop of a pilgrim's shell. And soon, mechanically, weary after a dull day with the prospect of a depressing morrow, I raised to my lips a spoonful of the tea in which I had soaked a morsel of the cake. No sooner had the warm liquid, and the crumbs with it, touched my palate than a shudder ran through my whole body, and I stopped, intent upon the extraordinary changes that were taking place. An exquisite pleasure had invaded my senses, but individual, detached, with no suggestion of its origin. And at once the vicissitudes of life had become indifferent to me, its disasters innocuous, its brevity illusory – this new sensation having had on me the effect which love has of filling me with a precious essence; or rather this essence was not in me, it was myself. . . . And suddenly the memory returns. The taste was that of the little crumb of madeleine which on Sunday mornings at Combray (because on those mornings I did not go out before church-time), when I went to say good day to her in her bedroom, my aunt Léonie used to give me, dipping it first in her own cup of real or of lime-flower tea. . . . And once I had recognized the taste of the crumb of madeleine soaked in her decoction of lime-flowers . . . immediately the old grey house upon the street, where her old room was, rose up like the scenery of a theatre . . .; and with the house the town, from morning to night and in all weathers, the Square where I was sent before luncheon, the streets along which I used to run errands, the country roads we took when it was fine. And just as the Japanese amuse themselves by filling a porcelain bowl with water and steeping in it little crumbs of paper which until then are without character or form, but, the moment they become flowers or houses or people, permanent and recognizable, so in that moment all the flowers in our garden and in M. Swann's park, and the water lilies on the Vivonne and the good folk of the village and their little dwellings and the parish church and the whole of Combray and of its surroundings, taking their proper shapes and growing solid, sprang into being, town and gardens alike, from my cup of tea.'

I, 58–62

A selection of moulds for madeleines, from *La Cuisinière de la campagne*, 1882.

The market-place at Illiers-
Combray. Photo Roger-Viollet.

Madeleines

	UK	US	
90 g	3 oz.	6 Tb	flour
	¼ tsp	¼ tsp	salt
	2	2	small eggs
90 g	3 oz.	⅓ cup	sugar
	½ tsp	½ tsp	vanilla essence or orangeflower extract
			grated rind of ½ lemon
90 g	3 oz.	¾ stick	unsalted butter
			icing/confectioners' sugar

Makes 18 small cakes

Melt the butter and let it cool to lukewarm. Set the oven to gas mark 4, 350° F. Sift the flour and salt together. Butter and flour the madeleine moulds. Beat the eggs, using an electric beater if desired, until thick and pale yellow. Add the vanilla or orangeflower extract and gradually beat in the sugar. Continue to beat until the mixture is very light and fluffy. Sprinkle on a third of the flour, lemon rind and butter at a time and fold in carefully with a rubber spatula so as not to lose the airiness of the mixture. Fill the moulds three-quarters full with the mixture.

Bake for 15 minutes. When cool turn out on to a cake rack and sprinkle with icing/confectioners' sugar.

Gâteau Manqué

This cake was so named when a baker whisked some egg whites badly for the cake he was preparing. Despite the mishap, the cake was well liked, and when he made it again the baker called it *manqué* (missed, failed). Nowadays the cake is baked in a *moule à manqué*, a mould with sloping sides created for this cake.

	UK	US	
90 g	3 oz.	¾ stick ¾ cup	butter
100 g	3½ oz.	+ 1 Tb	flour
			pinch of salt
30 g	1 oz.	2 Tb	ground almonds
	4	4	eggs
175 g	6 oz.	¾ cup	caster/fine sugar
	1½ Tb	1½ Tb	rum

glaze:

	UK	US	
230 ml	8 fl. oz.	1 cup	water
115 g	4 oz.	½ cup	sugar
		2 Tb	apricot jam rubbed through a sieve
			pralin or coarsely ground nuts

Serves 8

Set the oven to gas mark 4, 350° F. Melt the butter and let it cool to lukewarm. Butter and flour an 8-in. cake tin, preferably one with sloping sides (a *moule à manqué*), which will facilitate glazing.

Sieve the flour with the salt. Separate the eggs, placing the yolks in a larger bowl. Beat the egg yolks, using an electric beater if desired, and gradually add the sugar. Continue beating until the mixture is thick and very pale yellow. Stir in the rum, melted butter, ground almonds and finally the flour.

Beat the egg whites until stiff, stir a third into the cake mixture and fold in the rest. Pour into the cake tin and bake in the bottom third of the oven for 1 hour or until the cake begins to come away from the edge of the tin.

Unmould on to a cake rack when cool enough to handle.

Make the glaze by boiling together the water, sugar and jam until the syrup reaches the soft ball stage (240° F. on the sugar thermometer, see p. 125). Allow it to cool to below 200° F. or until it starts to thicken. Pour it over the cake, letting it drip down the sloping sides. Sprinkle a little pralin or some nuts on the top.

'. . . the ladies from the neighbouring country houses who on feast days, on their way through the market, would make the chickens cheep and the gossips stare, used to come to mass in their carriages. And they never returned home without buying from the pastrycook on the square . . . some of those cakes shaped like towers, protected from the sun by an awning – manqués, saint honorés, génoises – whose lingering sugary smell remains for me mingled with the sound of the bells for high mass and the gaiety of Sunday.'

Proust, Pastiches et mélanges

Macaroons · Massepains

Massepain, marchpane and marzipan are all forms of the same word (from the Italian *marzapane*) and refer to various sweetmeats based on ground almonds, from little marzipan fruits to macaroons.

	UK	US	
60 g	2 oz.	⅔ cup	ground almonds
90 g	3 oz.	6 Tb	caster/fine sugar
	1	1	egg white
	½ tsp	½ tsp	vanilla essence
	1	1	drop almond essence
	12	12	slivered almonds

Makes 12 macaroons

Set the oven to gas mark 6, 400° F.

Mix the ground almonds and sugar together well with the egg white, beating and stirring with a wooden spoon. Add the vanilla and almond essences. Form little round balls with a teaspoon and place them on a piece of rice paper on a baking sheet. Press a sliver of almond on top of each ball and bake for 15 minutes. When cool, cut off surplus rice paper and store in an airtight container.

Marcel tells about his uncle Adolphe:
'Once or twice every month, in Paris, I used to be sent to pay him a visit, as he was finishing his luncheon, wearing a plain alpaca coat, and waited upon by his servant in a working-jacket of striped linen, purple and white. He would complain that I had not been to see him for a long time, that he was being neglected; he would offer me a marchpane or a tangerine, and we would cross a room in which no one ever sat, ... And if we went to see him on certain days only, that was because on the other days ladies might come whom his family could not very well have met. ... one day I slipped out and ran all the way to his house. ... The manservant who let me in appeared embarrassed, and said my uncle was extremely busy ... I could hear my uncle grumbling and growing angry; finally the man-servant told me to come in.

'On the table was the same plate of marchpanes that was always there; my uncle wore the same alpaca coat as on other days; but opposite to him, in a pink silk dress with a great necklace of pearls about her throat, sat a young woman who was just finishing a tangerine.'

I, 96, 99, 100

Decorative panel from a pastrycook's shop front. Musée des Arts et Traditions Populaires, Paris.

Petits Fours

Petits fours is the general name given to a selection of miniature cakes, biscuits, glazed fruits and iced almond paste shapes that are served for *le goûter* (tea) in France.

The following recipe is for sponge cake, Génoise sponge, to be cut into little cakes and iced.

	UK	US	
	4	4	**eggs**
90 g	3 oz.	¾ cup	**icing/confectioners' sugar**
90 g	3 oz.	¾ stick	**unsalted butter**
		1 cup	
120 g	4 oz.	less 1 Tb	**flour**
			pinch of salt

'*I entered the Guermantes mansion . . . a butler who had long been in the service of the Prince de Guermantes having recognized me and brought to me in the library where I was waiting, so that I might not have to go to the buffet, a selection of petits fours and a glass of orangeade, I wiped my mouth with the napkin which he had given me; and instantly as though I had been the character in the Thousand and One Nights who unwittingly accomplishes the very rite which can cause to appear, visible to him alone, a docile genie ready to convey him to a great distance, a new vision of azure passed before my eyes.*'

XII, 225

Melt the butter gently and let it cool to lukewarm. Set the oven to gas mark 4, 350° F.

Sift the icing/confectioners' sugar on to a plate ready for use. Also sift the flour and salt together on to another plate ready for use. Line two 8-in. cake tins with buttered greaseproof paper.

Heat a large bowl by running hot water into it for a few minutes. Empty and dry the bowl, and place it on top of a saucepan of hot water over a very low heat. Break the eggs into it and beat, using an electric beater if desired, for 10 minutes, adding the sugar gradually after 5 minutes. (It is a good idea to sit down to this job.) The eggs and sugar will triple in size and become very light and airy.

Now remove the bowl from the saucepan, put it over a bowl of cold water and beat for another 5 minutes. Fold in the flour, a tablespoon at a time, with a rubber spatula, being very careful not to lose the airiness of the mixture. Fold in the butter carefully and pour the mixture into the cake tins. Bake in the bottom third of the oven for 40 minutes or until the edges of the cake come away from the sides of the tin and the cake rebounds when you make a depression in the top of it with your finger. (Avoid testing with a skewer, as the cake may fall.) Unmould on to a cake rack as soon as cool enough. Peel off the greaseproof paper and leave to cool completely.

To ice or glaze petits fours

Cut the sponge cake into tiny shapes such as squares, rectangles, diamonds or circles and, when ready to ice, place them on a cake rack above a baking sheet to catch the drippings. Two methods of icing or glazing are given opposite.

Fondant icing:

	UK	US	
350 g	12 oz.	1½ cups	sugar
175 ml	6 fl. oz.	¾ cup	water
	1 Tb	1 Tb	corn syrup or glucose to prevent sugar from crystallizing
			for flavouring:
			strong coffee
			melted chocolate
			lemon juice
			for garnish:
			walnut halves
			glacé cherries
			coconut

Cook the sugar, water and corn syrup or glucose together to the 'soft ball' stage (when some syrup dropped into cold water forms a soft ball) or 240° F. on the sugar thermometer. Brush a marble slab or counter with water, let the syrup cool for a minute and then pour it slowly on to the marble surface. With a flexible metal spatula pull the syrup to the centre, working all round, until it turns white. Gather it all together and reserve in a box or plastic bag.

When needed, put some of the fondant in a small saucepan, stir with a wooden spoon until warm and soft and add a teaspoon at a time of sugar syrup (see method below) until the mixture is liquid enough to spread. Add flavouring, such as 1 Tb strong coffee or 30 g/1 oz. melted chocolate. Stir thoroughly and pour over the little cakes, covering the tops and sides. Press on the walnut halves or pieces of glacé cherry or coconut if desired. Other methods of coating the cakes are by dipping them in the icing, holding them with tongs or a skewer, or spreading the icing on with a knife.

Glacé icing (glace au sucre):

	UK	US	
230 g	8 oz.	1 cup	sugar
115 ml	4 fl. oz.	½ cup	water
350 g	12 oz.	2½ cups	sifted icing/confectioners' sugar
			flavouring: see ingredients for fondant icing

Make a sugar syrup by boiling together the sugar and water for 10 minutes. When cool, add up to 350 g/12 oz./2½ cups sifted icing/confectioners' sugar, a spoonful at a time, stirring over very low heat until a smooth fluid icing is obtained. Add the desired flavouring and pour over the little cakes.

Biscuits Roses

	UK	US	
230 g	8 oz.	1¾ cups	flour
			pinch of salt
60 g	2 oz.	¼ cup	vanilla sugar (see p. 159)
60 g	2 oz.	½ stick	butter
	1	1	large egg
	1 tsp	1 tsp	orangeflower extract
			glacé icing (see recipe, p. 125)
			red food colouring

Makes approximately 24 plain tea biscuits

'"You are fond of hawthorns; just look at this pink one; isn't it pretty?" And it was indeed a hawthorn, but one whose flowers were pink and lovelier even than the white . . . it was attired even more richly than the rest, for the flowers which clung to its branches . . . were every one of them "in colour", and consequently of a superior quality, by the aesthetic standard of Combray, to the "plain", if one was to judge by the scale of prices at the "stores" in the Square, or at Camus's, where the most expensive biscuits were those whose sugar was pink.'

I, 190

Sift the flour and salt into a bowl. Slice the butter thinly and add it to the flour, rubbing it in with the tips of thumbs and fingers until a crumbly mixture is obtained. Add the sugar. Beat the egg lightly with a fork, and add to the mixture with the orangeflower extract. Stir with a fork until a rough dough is formed. Knead lightly, put in a plastic bag and chill for half an hour in the refrigerator.

Set the oven to gas mark 5, 375° F. Roll out the dough to a thickness of ⅛ in. on a floured board or counter and cut out biscuits with a small round cutter. Brush a baking sheet with water. Transfer the biscuits to the baking sheet with a spatula and bake for 20 minutes or until slightly brown.

Cool on a cake rack. Make glacé icing. Add 2 drops red food colouring, stir well, and add more colouring until the desired pink is obtained. Pour or spoon on top of each biscuit and leave to harden. Keep the biscuits in an airtight box.

Shortbread Fans · Sablés Normands

	UK	US	
		1 cup	
150 g	5 oz.	+ 1 Tb	flour
			pinch of salt
70 g	2½ oz.	½ cup	icing/confectioners' sugar
120 g	4 oz.	1 stick	butter
40 g	1½ oz.	1½ Tb	ground almonds
	2	2	egg yolks
			icing/confectioners' sugar

Makes about 15 fans

'Already, during the 1914 war, he had given up croissants and never took to them again. I tried instead to tempt his failing appetite with sablés. I had been told about a high-class cook who made excellent ones. He made me some to order; they were delicious. I arranged them on the plate; M. Proust sampled them and asked where they had come from. He then said: "Thank the man for his trouble and thank you too, dear Céleste, for having thought of them." But he didn't want any.'

CA, 94

Sift the flour with the salt and sugar. Add the ground almonds and the butter, cut in pieces, and rub together to form a crumbly mixture. Make a well in this mixture, put in the egg yolks and stir with a fork, forming into a coherent mass as quickly as possible. Put in a plastic bag in the refrigerator for 1 hour.

Set the oven to gas mark 6, 400° F. Roll out the pastry on a floured board or counter to a thickness of ⅛ in. Using a round cutter, cut 3½ in.-diameter circles in the pastry and with a knife cut each round into thirds. Butter a baking sheet and transfer the biscuits to the sheet with a metal spatula. Shape into fans by giving each point a squeeze with thumb and forefinger. With the blunt edge of a small knife, mark off the spines of the fan and a small circle near the point.

Bake for 10 minutes, allow to cool for 5 minutes, then remove the biscuits with the spatula to a cake rack. Sprinkle with icing sugar, and when completely cool store in an airtight container.

Norman Puff Pastries · Feuilletés Normands

	UK	US	
230 g	½ lb.	½ lb.	puff pastry (see recipe, p. 156, or frozen)
	4	4	Golden Delicious (or similar) apples
30 g	1 oz.	¼ stick	butter
30 g	1 oz.	2 Tb	sugar
	1 Tb	1 Tb	Calvados
	4 Tb	4 Tb	*crème anglaise* (see recipe, p. 159) or double/heavy cream extra sugar to sprinkle over pastry
	1	1	egg, beaten
	1 tsp	1 tsp	milk

Makes 8

Quarter, peel and core the apples and chop them into small cubes. Melt the butter in a saucepan and add the apples, sugar and Calvados. Cook over medium heat for 10 minutes, until the apples have lost most of their crispness but have not yet begun to break up.

Set the oven to gas mark 7, 425° F. Roll out pastry to a large rectangle approximately 16 in. by 8 in. and ⅛ in. thick. Divide the rectangle into 8 squares. Put a tablespoon of apple in the middle of each square and top it with half a tablespoon of *crème anglaise* or cream.

Wet edges of pastry with water and fold on the diagonal. Press together and make small indentations with a knife along the edges. Prick three or four small holes in the top of each pastry, brush with the beaten egg mixed with 1 teaspoon of milk, and sprinkle with sugar.

Bake for 25 minutes or until the pastry is puffed up and golden in colour.

'. . . to partake of the rock cakes, Norman puff pastry, tartlets shaped like boats filled with cherries . . .'

VIII, 202

'Les Galettes' by Claude Monet, 1882 (detail). Durand Ruel.

'But since they were having luncheon late . . . only the large apple tart was served, a tart that looked as yellow as the door of the General Shop on the Square but covered in a sauce as red as the flowers of the pink hawthorn which grew round the porch of the church opposite the shop upon the Square. It was definitely a Sunday tart, gazed at with admiration and eaten with relish on those Sunday noons, with the narrow street outside on the same level as the room and sky purplish-blue when the weather was stormy, or a-flicker with gold when the sun was shining.'
Jean Santeuil, 175

Golden Delicious apples, drawn by Alice B. Ellis.

Apple Tart · Tarte aux Pommes

	UK	US	
450 g	1 lb.	1 lb.	sweet pastry (see recipe, p. 114)
	8	8	apples (Golden Delicious)
	3 Tb	3 Tb	apricot jam
30 g	1 oz.	¼ stick	unsalted butter
	3 Tb	3 Tb	redcurrant jelly or apricot jam *plus*
	1 Tb	1 Tb	Calvados or juice of ½ lemon as glaze
	1 Tb	1 Tb	toasted slivered almonds (see method, p. 112)

Serves 8–10

Prepare the sweet pastry and chill in the refrigerator for half an hour. Roll out on to a floured board or counter, to a 10-inch square. Roll the pastry around the rolling pin and unroll it onto a baking sheet. Alternatively roll out the pastry to fit a 12-inch quiche or pie dish.

Pinch the edges with your fingertips to form a fluted edge. Set the oven to gas mark 6, 400° F. Prick the pastry with a fork and cover with a sheet of aluminium foil, with dried beans on top, so that it keeps its shape while baking. Bake for 20 minutes in the top third of the oven, removing the foil and beans after 15 minutes. Let the pastry cool.

Spread 3 tablespoons of apricot jam over it. Quarter the apples and peel and core them. Slice each quarter into very thin slices (approximately 6 slices to each quarter). Arrange on the pastry in rows, if the tart is square, or in a circle if it is round, the slices lying slightly slanted and overlapping.

Melt the butter and brush it over the apple slices; sprinkle with sugar. Cover edges of pastry with strips of aluminium foil and put under a pre-heated grill/broiler to brown the top edges of the apple slices, moving the tart around and masking them with aluminium foil as they brown, until the browning is completed.

To glaze the tart, melt either the redcurrant jelly and Calvados or the apricot jam/preserve and Calvados or lemon juice together, and strain into a bowl. Brush this glaze over the apple slices and sprinkle with toasted almond slivers. If the tart was prepared on a baking sheet, cut into portions and arrange on a serving dish.

Strawberry Tartlets · Tartes aux Fraises

	UK	US	
450 g	1 lb.	1 lb.	sweet pastry (see recipe, p. 114. Replace 3 oz. of the total flour with 3 oz. ground almonds)
1.1 kg	2½ lb.	2½ lb.	strawberries
450 g	1 lb.	1 lb.	redcurrant jelly (approximately)

optional base:

180 g	6 oz.	6 oz.	cream cheese
	2 Tb	2 Tb	single/light cream
	2 Tb	2 Tb	icing/confectioners' sugar
			grated rind of ¼ lemon
150 ml	¼ pint	⅔ cup	double/heavy cream (optional)

Makes 8–10

'No doubt the Princess was fully prepared to admit that it was possible to derive more enjoyment in the company of the Duchesse de Guermantes than in her own. . . . And in vain might she commit to memory Oriane's witty sayings, copy her gowns, serve at her own tea-parties the same strawberry tarts, there were occasions on which she was left by herself all afternoon with a lady in waiting and some foreign Counsellor of Legation.'

VI, 205–6

Note. These tarts can be filled simply with the strawberries and a redcurrant glaze, or with a cream cheese or *crème anglaise* base (see recipe above or p. 159). Use tartlet moulds of approximately 3½ in. diameter.

Prepare the sweet pastry and chill it for half an hour in the refrigerator. Roll out to a thickness of ⅛ in. Set the oven to gas mark 6, 400° F. Cut out rounds slightly larger than the tartlet moulds. Press the pastry into the moulds and fill with pieces of crushed aluminium foil, so that the tartlets keep their shape during baking. Bake for 20 minutes, removing the foil after 15 minutes. Let cool.

For a cream cheese base, rub the cream cheese through a nylon sieve, add the single/light cream, sugar and lemon rind and mix well. Spread over the bottom of the pastry.

Wash the strawberries if necessary and hull them. Arrange them tip end up on the cream cheese base. Melt the redcurrant jelly, strain into a little bowl and brush or pour it over the strawberries. Halve the strawberries if they are very large.

Decorate with cream if desired.

Apricot Tart · Tarte aux Abricots

	UK	US	
230 g	½ lb.	½ lb.	sweet pastry (half amount of recipe on p. 114)
680 g	1½ lb.	1½ lb.	fresh apricots *or*
	2 medium	2 medium	
	tins	cans	apricot halves
	3 Tb	3 Tb	apricot jam
	1 Tb	1 Tb	sugar
	1 Tb	1 Tb	kirsch
	½ Tb	½ Tb	toasted almond slivers (see method for toasting, p. 112)

sugar syrup (if fresh apricots are used):

230 ml	8 fl. oz.	1 cup	water
120 g	4 oz.	½ cup	sugar

Serves 6

'We would climb to the highest point of the cliff, and, when we had reached it and were seated on the grass, would undo our parcel of sandwiches and cakes. My friends preferred the sandwiches, and were surprised to see me eat only a single chocolate cake, sugared with gothic tracery, or an apricot tart. This was because, with the sandwiches of cheese and salad, a form of food that was novel to me and knew nothing of the past, I had nothing in common. But the cakes understood, the tarts were gossips. There were in the former an insipid taste of cream, in the latter a fresh taste of fruit which knew all about Combray, and about Gilberte . . .'

IV, 283–4

Prepare the sweet pastry and chill in the refrigerator for half an hour. Roll out on a floured board or counter to fit a 9-inch quiche or pie dish. Roll the pastry round the rolling pin and unroll it on to the dish. Pinch the edges with fingertips to form a fluted edge. If individual tarts are required, fill 3½-inch tartlet moulds with pastry, as in strawberry tart recipe, p. 129.

Set the oven to gas mark 6, 400° F. Prick the pastry with a fork and cover with aluminium foil, with dried beans on top, so that the pastry keeps its shape while baking. Bake for 20 minutes in the top third of the oven, removing the foil and beans after 15 minutes. Leave to cool.

If using fresh apricots, halve and pit them. To make a sugar syrup, bring the water and sugar to the boil in a saucepan large enough to take the apricots in one layer. Place the apricots, rounded side down, in the syrup and poach over low heat until tender – the exact cooking time depends on the ripeness of the fruit. Remove with a slotted spoon and reserve. If using tinned/canned apricots, drain and reserve.

Spread 1½ tablespoons of apricot jam on to the pastry, then lay the apricot halves, rounded side down, in overlapping circles. Sprinkle with the sugar. Cover the edges of the pastry with strips of foil and place under a pre-heated grill/broiler to brown the tops of the apricots.

Melt the remaining apricot jam with the kirsch, strain into a bowl and brush it over the apricots.

Sprinkle with toasted almond slivers.

Cherry Tartlets · Barquettes aux Cerises

	UK	US	
230 g	8 oz.	1¾ cup	flour
30 g	1 oz.	¼ cup	icing/confectioners' sugar
	½ tsp	½ tsp	salt
120 g	4 oz.	1 stick	butter
	4 Tb	4 Tb	water

filling:

700 g	1½ lb.	1½ lb.	cherries* *or*
	2 medium tins	2 medium cans	cherries
230 g	½ lb.	½ lb.	cherry jam or blackcurrant jelly *plus*
	1 Tb	1 Tb	kirsch

Makes 18

Using the above ingredients, make pastry as on page 114. Leave it to chill for half an hour. Lightly butter 18 little barquette moulds. Roll out the pastry to a thickness of ⅛ inch, cut out pieces slightly larger than the moulds and line the moulds with the pastry. Prick with a fork.

Set the oven to gas mark 6, 400° F. Press small pieces of crushed aluminium foil onto the pastry so that it keeps its shape during baking. Place the barquette moulds on 2 baking sheets. Bake for 20 minutes in all, removing the foil after 15 minutes. If the pastry has risen press it back into shape with the foil while it is still warm. Let cool. Invert the pastries on to a cake rack.

Wash, stem and pit the cherries and arrange them in the barquettes. Halve the cherries if they are very large. Melt the cherry jam or blackcurrant jelly with the kirsch, strain into a bowl and spoon over the cherries. Try to do this not longer than 2 hours before serving so that the pastry remains crisp.

* Choose sweet pink cherries when in season; other cherries can of course be used and tinned/canned black or morello cherries can be substituted for the fresh cherries in wintertime.

Included in the tea party at La Raspelière: 'tartlets shaped like boats filled with cherries like beads of coral.'
VIII, 202

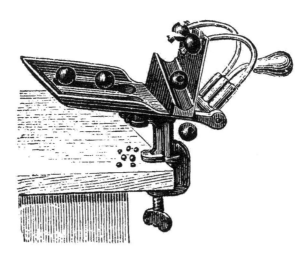

Cherry-stoning tool. From *Grand livre des pâtissiers et des confiseurs* by Urbain Dubois.

In Jean Santeuil *there is a description of a Sunday lunch that ends with large dishes filled with grapes, others with fruits and more plates of biscuits like macaroons and* langues de chat.

Jean Santeuil, 353

In the pâtisserie.

'*The wit of the Guermantes – a thing as nonexistent as the squared circle, according to the Duchess who regarded herself as the sole Guermantes to possess it – was a family of reputation like that of the rillettes de Tours or the biscuits of Rheims.*'

VI, 207

Cats' Tongues · Langues de Chat

	UK	US	
60 g	2 oz.	½ stick	butter
60 g	2 oz.	½ cup	icing/confectioners' sugar
60 g	2 oz.	scant ½ cup	flour
	2	2	egg whites
	1 tsp	1 tsp	vanilla essence

Makes 24

Set the oven to gas mark 6, 400° F. Cream the butter in a bowl, using an electric beater if desired, and gradually add the icing sugar and flour; when soft, add the egg whites and vanilla essence. Butter a baking sheet. Fill a pastry bag with the dough and force it through a ⅛-in. nozzle, in 2½-in. strips, 1½ in. apart from each other. Bake for 5 to 6 minutes or until they have spread out and are light brown around the edges and white in the middle.

Biscuits de Reims

	UK	US	
	3	3	large eggs
125 g	4 oz.	½ cup	vanilla sugar
150 g	5 oz.	1 cup + 1 Tb	flour
			pinch of salt
			red food colouring
			icing/confectioners' sugar to dust the cakes

Makes approximately 24 little dry cakes, suitable for serving with tea or coffee, or traditionally to dip in champagne.

Set the oven to gas mark 4, 350° F. Butter and dust with sugar 3½-inch rectangular moulds or other available little cake moulds.

Separate the eggs. Beat the yolks with an electric beater until light; then gradually add the sugar and continue beating until the mixture is thick and nearly white. Add drops of red colouring until the mixture is dark pink.

Sieve the flour with the salt and put aside. Beat the egg whites until stiff. Stir a tablespoon of the whites into the yolks and sugar, then fold in the rest. Fold in the flour, sprinkling on about a quarter of it at a time, being careful to keep the airiness of the mixture.

Spoon the dough into the moulds, filling them half full, as they will expand while baking. Bake for 20 minutes without opening the oven door.

Let the cakes cool for 10 minutes, then turn out on to a cake rack and dust with icing/confectioners' sugar.

Desserts and Ices

'A dessert course without cheese is like a pretty woman with only one eye' – Brillat-Savarin. Drawing from *L'Art de bien manger* by E. Richardin, 1910.

'After first nibbling a pink biscuit, Jean would crush his strawberries into a portion of cream cheese until the resultant colour gave promise of the taste long dreamed of and now, in a moment or two, to become a reality. Meanwhile, he would add a few more strawberries and a scrap more cream, in carefully calculated proportion, pleasure fighting with concentration in his eyes, with all the accumulated experience of a colourist and the intuition of an epicure.'

Jean Santeuil, 139

Albertine on the street cries of Paris: ' "Oh dear, it's the same with the little hearts of cream cheese, such a long time to wait : 'Bon fromage à la cré, à la cré, bon fromage.' " '

IX, 167

Cream Cheese · Fromage à la Crème

It is quite simple to make your own cream cheese. It is delicious and for 4 people you require:

	UK	US	
1½ litres	2½ pints	1½ quarts	rich *unhomogenized milk*

Put the milk in a bowl or jug and leave in a warm place until it sours and becomes solid and the curd and whey separate. This might take up to 2 days. If the milk is very rich, you will have to skim the butter off the top of the curd. Drain the curd into a piece of cheesecloth or muslin approximately 20 inches square. Tie opposite corners of the cloth together to form a bag, drape it over a ½-litre/1-pint/2½-cup carafe bottle (or similar) and set in a bowl. Leave to drain for 12 hours or overnight in a refrigerator. This produces approximately 375 g/13 oz./1½ cups of cream cheese. If the cheese becomes dry and crumbly, push it through a sieve and stir in some cream or milk to soften the texture.

Pink cream cheese

	UK	US	
375 g	13 oz.	1½ cups	cream cheese (recipe as above)
250 g	½ lb.	3 cups	strawberries
			milk or cream

Hull the strawberries and rinse. Crush with a wooden spoon or fork. Mix thoroughly with the cream cheese and a little milk or cream. To obtain a really smooth cream, rub the mixture through a nylon sieve with a wooden spoon. Delicious as it is – or sprinkle with sugar.

Cream Cheese Hearts · Cœurs à la Crème

	UK	US	
230 g	8 oz.	8 oz.	curd cheese (ricotta)
230 g	8 oz.	8 oz.	cream cheese (see recipe above)
			pinch of salt
230 ml	8 fl. oz.	1 cup	double/heavy cream

Serves 6

Rub the cheeses through a sieve with a wooden spoon, add the salt and cream and whisk until smooth. Turn into little china heart-shaped moulds with draining holes. Allow to drain onto a large dish in the refrigerator overnight. Unmould and sprinkle with sugar, if desired.

The appropriate moulds are available in most good kitchen shops, but the cheeses may of course be drained in any suitable réceptacle. They are delicious with strawberries.

Rice à l'Impératrice

	UK	US	
200 g	7 oz.	1 cup	dessert rice
570 ml	1 pint	2½ cups	milk
	½	½	vanilla pod split lengthwise
60 g	2 oz.	¼ cup	sugar
60 g	2 oz.	⅓ cup	glacé/candied orange and lemon peel soaked in kirsch, marc, or rum
	2 Tb	2 Tb	apricot jam
			grated rind of 1 lemon
	1 Tb	1 Tb	gelatin
			juice of 1 orange

custard:

	3	3	egg yolks
30 g	1 oz.	2 Tb	vanilla sugar
300 ml	½ pint	1¼ cups	milk
			pinch of salt
150 ml	¼ pint	⅔ cup	double/heavy cream
	3 Tb	3 Tb	redcurrant jelly

Serves 8

'Since my parents had told me that, for my first visit to the theatre, I should have to choose between these two pieces, I would study exhaustively and in turn the title of one and the title of the other (for those were all that I knew of either), . . . I was as little capable of deciding which play I should prefer to see as if, at the dinner table, they had obliged me to choose between rice à l'Impératrice, and the famous cream of chocolate.'

I, 97–98

Put the rice, milk, vanilla pod and sugar in the top of a double boiler. Cover and cook over simmering water for 1 hour until the rice is tender and the milk absorbed completely. Remove the vanilla pod. In the meantime stir the gelatin into the orange juice in a little bowl, and place the bowl over simmering water for a few minutes until the gelatin is completely dissolved. Put aside to cool.

Make a custard by heating the milk gently in a saucepan. Beat the egg yolks in a bowl, using an electric beater if desired, adding a pinch of salt and then the vanilla sugar. When the mixture is thick and creamy, add the milk, lowering the speed of the beater. Scrape the sides well and pour the mixture back into the saucepan. Stir this mixture over low heat until it thickens and coats the back of the spoon. Add the gelatin and juice and stir well. Pour the custard through a sieve into a bowl and leave to cool, whisking occasionally to prevent a skin forming.

When the rice and custard are cool, mix them together with the finely chopped candied peel, the apricot jam and grated lemon rind. Whip the cream until stiff and fold it into the mixture. Boil the redcurrant jelly and stir until smooth. Lightly oil a brioche or ring mould or mould of your choice and strain in the redcurrant jelly to coat the bottom. Spoon in the rice mixture and leave to set for 4 hours or more in the refrigerator.

To unmould, invert the mould onto a dish, wet a teacloth with hot water, wring out and place on the mould; repeat if necessary. This dish can be garnished with vanilla pears (see Poire Bourdaloue recipe, p. 138), apricots or peaches.

Chocolate Cream · Crème de Chocolat

	UK	US	
175 g	6 oz.	6 squares	plain or semi-sweet chocolate – Menier, Bournville or Baker's
½ litre	18 fl. oz.	2¼ cups	milk
115 ml	4 fl. oz.	½ cup	double/heavy cream
45 g	1½ oz.	3 Tb	caster/fine sugar
	4	4	egg yolks
	¾ tsp	¾ tsp	vanilla essence
115 ml	4 fl. oz.	½ cup	single/light cream
			freshly grated nutmeg or cinnamon

Makes 8 petits pots or ramekins of 125 ml/4 fl. oz./½ cup capacity

Set the oven to gas mark 3, 325° F.

Break up the chocolate and melt it in the milk over low heat until nearly boiling. Stir well, making sure all the chocolate has dissolved. Beat the egg yolks, using an electric beater if desired, and gradually add the sugar, beating, until the mixture is thick and pale-coloured. When the milk and chocolate mixture is hot, pour half the amount onto the egg yolks, carefully, to avoid splashing. Now add this mixture to the rest of the milk and chocolate in the saucepan; add the vanilla essence and double/heavy cream and stir well. Strain into a jug and pour into the ramekins or *petits pots*. Place in a roasting pan or oven dish with a little hot water covering the bottom of the pan and cook for 35 minutes. Take out and leave to cool.

Chill for several hours or overnight and just before serving cover with a layer of cream and sprinkle with freshly grated nutmeg or cinnamon.

Chocolate Soufflé · Soufflé au Chocolat

	UK	US	
30 g	1 oz.	¼ stick	butter
30 g	1 oz.	4 Tb	flour
230 ml	8 fl. oz.	1 cup	milk
175 g	6 oz.	6 squares	Menier, Bournville, or Baker's semi-sweet chocolate
	6	6	eggs
			pinch of salt
	1 Tb	1 Tb	cognac or Cointreau
175 g	6 fl. oz.	¾ cup	single/light cream

Serves 6 (7½ in. soufflé dish, 1.5 litre/2½ pint/6 cup capacity)

Break up the chocolate into small pieces. Melt the butter in a saucepan over low heat, add the flour and mix well off the heat. Add the milk, stir until thick and smooth, and simmer for 5 minutes over very low heat, stirring occasionally. Add the chocolate and stir until melted. Take off the heat and pour into a large bowl. Let cool.

Set the oven to gas mark 5, 375° F. Place a baking sheet on the middle oven shelf to pre-heat. Butter a soufflé dish and dust with sugar.

Separate the eggs and whisk the yolks and the cognac or Cointreau into the chocolate mixture. Beat the egg whites with a pinch of salt until stiff. Stir a quarter of them into the soufflé base and carefully fold in the rest. Pour into the soufflé dish and bake on the pre-heated baking sheet for 25–30 minutes. The hot baking sheet will help the soufflé to rise well. The inside of the soufflé should be creamy and the flavour will be enhanced by pouring over single/light cream.

Dinner at the Verdurins' : '"What is this charmingly coloured thing that we are eating?" asked Ski. "It is called strawberry mousse," said Mme Verdurin, "But it is ex-qui-site. You ought to open bottles of Château-Margaux, Château-Lafite, port wine." "I can't tell you how he amuses me, he never drinks anything but water," said Mme Verdurin, seeking to cloak with her delight at such a flight of fancy her alarm at the thought of so prodigal an outlay.'

VIII, 118

Strawberry Mousse · Mousse à la Fraise

	UK	US	
350 g	12 oz.	2½ cups	strawberries, fresh or frozen
			juice of 1 lemon
	2 Tb	2 Tb	water
	1 Tb	1 Tb	gelatin (1 envelope)
90 g	3 oz.	6 Tb	caster/fine sugar
175 ml	6 fl. oz.	¾ cup	double/heavy cream
	2	2	large egg whites *or*
	3	3	small egg whites
			pinch of salt

to decorate:

150 ml	¼ pint	⅔ cup	double/heavy cream
			extra strawberries

Serves 6

Wash, drain and hull the strawberries. If using frozen strawberries, defrost them in the refrigerator until they are just soft and use right away, before they become mushy and discoloured. Liquidize or mash the strawberries, with a wooden spoon. Add the sugar. Stir the gelatin into the lemon juice and water in a little bowl or cup; place the bowl over simmering water and stir until dissolved. Add this mixture to the strawberries.

Using an electric beater if desired, whip the cream until firm, add the strawberry mixture and beat until stiff. Place the mixture in the refrigerator for half an hour to an hour or until quite thick and the gelatin is beginning to set. Beat the egg whites with a pinch of salt until stiff and stir a tablespoonful into the mixture. Then fold in the rest with a rubber spatula. Pour into a soufflé dish of 1¾-pint (1 US quart) capacity. Chill for 4 hours. Decorate with extra strawberries and whipped cream, if desired.

Bourdaloue Pear · Poire Bourdaloue

	UK	US	
	8	8	unripe pears
570 ml	1 pint	2½ cups	water
60 g	2 oz.	¼ cup	sugar
	1½ tsp	1½ tsp	vanilla essence
			juice of ½ lemon

Bourdaloue custard:

	UK	US	
570 ml	1 pint	2½ cups	milk
	4	4	egg yolks
230 g	8 oz.	1¾ cups	icing/confectioners' sugar
30 g	1 oz.	4 Tb	rice flour *or* flour
	¼ tsp	¼ tsp	salt
			drop of almond essence
	1 tsp	1 tsp	vanilla essence
30 g	1 oz.	¼ stick	unsalted butter
	1 Tb	1 Tb	kirsch or marc
	2 Tb	2 Tb	toasted slivered almonds

Serves 8

' "*Céleste, I should like something chocolaty.*" "*What sort of thing, sir?*" "*You choose*".

'*Sometimes it would be ten or eleven in the evening when he asked me. I would run down to Latinville, rue La Boétie, which fortunately stayed open late, and bring back a sweet . . . He would eat one or two teaspoonfuls and that would be all.*

'*Another time I would order a Bourdaloue pear from the Restaurant Larue. The same thing used to happen.*'

CA, 102

Make a syrup by simmering the water, sugar and vanilla together in a large heavy saucepan until the sugar dissolves.

The pears named Doyenné des Comices are suitable for this dish. Peel the pears with a potato peeler and squeeze lemon juice on them to prevent discoloration. Halve them and cut away the core. Put into the hot syrup and cook over medium heat for about half an hour or until tender. Let them cool in the syrup.

Custard

Heat the milk. Sift the sugar with the rice flour and the salt. Beat the egg yolks in a bowl, using an electric beater if desired, and gradually add the sugar, flour and salt and finally the hot milk. Now return this mixture to the saucepan and stir constantly with a wooden spoon over low heat until the mixture thickens and coats the back of the spoon. Add the almond and vanilla essences and the butter cut into thin slices. Stir until the butter melts, strain into a bowl and put to cool.

When the pears and custard are cool, lay the halves on a dish, mix the liqueur into the custard with a whisk and coat the pears with it. Pound the almonds a little in a mortar and sprinkle over the top. Chill.

The pears and custard may be served on a base of sponge cake or in a tart.

Chestnut Purée · Purée de Marrons

To garnish the dessert called Mont Blanc or to serve with cream or ice cream.

	UK	US	
450 g	1 lb.	1 lb.	chestnuts
150 ml	¼ pint	⅔ cup	milk
150 ml	¼ pint	⅔ cup	water
			pinch of salt

sugar syrup:

	UK	US	
300 ml	½ pint	1¼ cups	water
60 g	2 oz.	¼ cup	sugar
	½ tsp	½ tsp	vanilla essence

Cook the chestnuts as in the recipe for unsweetened chestnut purée (p. 89), but strain them and pour away any liquid. Make a syrup by boiling the sugar and water together for 10–15 minutes until reduced to approximately 75 ml/ 3 fl. oz./7–8 Tb sugar syrup. Take this off the heat and let it cool. Push the chestnuts through the fine mesh of the food mill twice and stir in the syrup and vanilla essence. Dry the mixture out, as in the recipe for the unsweetened version, if needed as a garnish for a dessert like Mont Blanc, where the chestnuts must have the appearance of vermicelli. This is achieved by pushing through the medium mesh of the food mill.

Chocolate Ice Cream · Glace au Chocolat

From Albertine's rhapsody on ices:
' "*Oh dear, at the Ritz I'm afraid you'll find Vendôme Columns of ice, chocolate ice or raspberry, and then you will need a lot of them so that they may look like votive pillars or pylons erected along an avenue to the glory of Coolness.*"'

IX, 169

	UK	US	
750 ml	1¼ pints	3¼ cups	milk
230 g	8 oz.	8 squares	plain chocolate, Menier, Bournville or Baker's semi-sweet
	5	5	egg yolks
			pinch of salt
45 g	1½ oz.	3 Tb	caster/fine sugar
	1 tsp	1 tsp	vanilla essence
300 ml	½ pint	1¼ cups	double/heavy cream

Break the chocolate into pieces and heat with the milk in the top of a double boiler until very hot and the chocolate has melted thoroughly. Strain through a layer of cheesecloth, if necessary gathering up and squeezing with the hands to hasten the process.

Beat the yolks and a pinch of salt, using an electric beater if desired, and gradually add the sugar, beating until the mixture is thick and pale yellow. Pour the hot milk carefully onto the yolks, slowing down the speed of the beater and scraping the sides of the bowl with a spatula. Now pour the mixture back into the top of the double boiler and stir constantly with a wooden spoon over medium heat until the custard thickens and coats the back of the spoon. Be careful, for this custard can curdle and separate, so avoid over-heating and have patience! When it is thick, stir in the vanilla essence, pour through a sieve into a bowl and let it cool, whisking occasionally to prevent a skin forming on the top. If the mixture does curdle, quickly pour through a sieve into a clean saucepan. Beat another egg yolk in a bowl and sieve the mixture in, little by little, constantly beating, thereby rebuilding the emulsion. Refrigerate the mixture.

Beat the cream until stiff, and fold into the cool custard. Freeze in an electric ice cream freezer or the churn type freezer, pouring into a lightly oiled mould before it sets completely. Freeze for 2 or more hours or until thoroughly frozen. This ice cream freezes quite smoothly without being churned, because of the addition of the whipped cream.

Remove from the refrigerator 15 minutes before serving. To unmould, invert the mould onto a dish and cover it with a hot damp cloth for a minute or so.

Raspberry Ice Cream · Glace à la Framboise

	UK	US	
350 g	12 oz.	2½ cups	raspberries
			juice of ½ lemon
120 g	4 oz.	1 cup	icing/confectioners' sugar
300 ml	½ pint	1¼ cups	double/heavy cream
	2	2	large eggs *or* 3 small
			pinch salt
	½ tsp	½ tsp	cream of tartar

Serves 8

' "They make raspberry obelisks too, which will rise up here and there in the burning desert of my thirst, and I shall make their pink granite crumble and melt deep down in my throat which they will refresh better than any oasis." '

IX, 169

When fresh raspberries are not available, use frozen fruit or good-quality canned ones.

If frozen raspberries are used, defrost them. Canned ones should be drained and the sugar omitted from the recipe.

Rub the raspberries through a sieve with a wooden spoon and discard the pips. Add the lemon juice and sugar. Using an electric beater if desired, beat the egg whites with the salt and cream of tartar until stiff but not dry. In another bowl but using the same beater (saves washing up), whip the cream until thick and floppy. Add the raspberry purée and continue to beat until the mixture is firm. With a rubber spatula or large metal spoon, fold in the egg whites.

Pour the mixture into a lightly oiled mould. Freeze for 2 hours or longer, until quite firm.

To turn out the ice cream, invert the mould on to a serving dish and wrap it for a few seconds, just long enough to loosen the contents, in a cloth wrung out of hot water. Lift off the mould and serve immediately.

Moulds for making ice cream.

' "*Those mountains of ice at the Ritz sometimes suggest Monte Rosa, and indeed, if it is a lemon ice, I do not object to its not having a monumental shape, its being irregular, abrupt, like one of Elstir's mountains. It ought not to be too white then, but slightly yellowish, with that look of dull, dirty snow that Elstir's mountains have. The ice need not be at all big, only half an ice if you like, those lemon ices are still mountains, reduced to a tiny scale, but our imagination restores their dimensions, . . . at the foot of my yellowish lemon ice, I can see quite clearly postillions, travellers, post-chaises over which my tongue sets to work to roll down freezing avalanches that will swallow them up.*" '

IX, 169–70

Lemon Ice Cream · Glace au Citron

	UK	US	
	2	2	egg whites
230 g	8 oz.	1 cup	sugar
175 ml	6 fl. oz.	¾ cup	water
300 ml	½ pint	1¼ cups	single/light cream
150 ml	¼ pint	⅔ cup	milk
			pinch of salt
150 ml	¼ pint	⅔ cup	lemon juice (4 lemons)
			grated rind of 1 lemon

Serves 6. Makes 1 litre/1¾ pints/1 US quart

Make a sugar syrup by boiling together the sugar and water for 5 minutes. Let it cool a little. Beat the egg whites until stiff and pour in the syrup gradually, continuing to beat. Stir in the rest of the ingredients and freeze in an electric ice-cream freezer or churn-type freezer. Pour into a mould of your choice before it freezes completely. Freeze for 2 or more hours or until thoroughly frozen. To serve, invert the mould onto a dish and cover with a hot damp cloth for a few minutes.

Strawberry Ice Cream · Glace à la Fraise

	UK	US	
350 g	12 oz.	2½ cups	strawberries, fresh or frozen
			juice of ½ lemon
90 g	3 oz.	⅔ cup	caster/fine sugar
300 ml	½ pint	1¼ cups	double/heavy cream
	2	2	large egg whites *or*
	3	3	small egg whites
			pinch of salt
	½ tsp	½ tsp	cream of tartar

Serves 8

' "*I set my lips to work to destroy, pillar after pillar, those Venetian churches of a porphyry that is made with strawberries, and send what I spare of them crashing down upon the worshippers.*" '

IX, 170

Wash, drain and hull the strawberries. If using frozen strawberries, defrost them in the refrigerator until they are just soft and use right away, before they become mushy and discoloured. Mash the strawberries with a wooden spoon and add the lemon juice and sugar.

Using an electric beater if desired, beat the whites until stiff, with salt and cream of tartar. Then whip the cream until firm, add the strawberry mixture and continue to beat until stiff. Fold in the egg whites with a rubber spatula and freeze in an electric ice-cream freezer or churn-type freezer, pouring into a lightly oiled mould (capacity 1 litre/1¾ pint/1 US quart) before it sets completely. Freeze for 2 or more hours or until thoroughly frozen. This ice cream freezes quite smoothly without being churned, because of the addition of whipped cream and egg whites, but churning is recommended because the texture becomes even creamier. To serve, invert the mould onto a dish and cover with a damp hot cloth for a few minutes.

Coffee and Pistachio Ice Cream ·
Glace au Café et à la Pistache

The coffee and pistachio ice creams are made separately, and can fill a bombe mould or a savarin mould. The bombe mould is coated with coffee ice cream and filled with pistachio ice cream; this is called Bombe Joséphine. It is advisable to read the recipe through before starting preparations. Alternatively the ice creams can be poured in two layers into a savarin mould. Each of these ice creams serves 8 people – the two together, 16.

Coffee Ice Cream

	UK	US	
750 ml	1¼ pints	3¼ cups	milk
90 g	3 oz.	6 heaped Tb	finely ground after-dinner coffee (Continental blend preferred)
	5	5	egg yolks
			pinch of salt
150 g	5 oz.	⅔ cup	caster/fine sugar
300 ml	½ pint	1¼ cup	double/heavy cream
25 g	1 Tb	1 Tb	toasted slivered almonds for decoration

Heat the milk with the ground coffee until it comes to the boil. Remove from the heat, stir and let the coffee settle. Strain through a layer of cheesecloth, gathering up and squeezing with the hands if necessary, to hasten the procedure. Pour the milk and coffee mixture into the top of a double boiler over simmering water. Stir half the sugar into the milk. Beat the yolks and a pinch of salt, using an electric beater if desired, and gradually add the rest of the sugar, beating until the mixture is thick and pale yellow. Pour half the hot milk carefully onto the yolks, slowing down the speed of the beater and scraping the sides of the bowl with a spatula. Now pour the whole mixture back into the top of the double boiler and stir constantly with a wooden spoon over simmering water until the custard thickens and coats the back of the spoon. Be careful, for this custard can curdle and separate, so avoid over-heating and have patience! When the custard is thick enough, pour through a sieve and let it cool, whisking occasionally to prevent a skin forming on the top. If the mixture does curdle, quickly pour through a sieve into a clean saucepan. Beat an egg yolk in another bowl and pour the mixture through a sieve onto the yolk, beating continuously and thereby rebuilding the emulsion.

Beat the cream until stiff, and fold into the cool custard. Freeze in an electric ice-cream freezer or a churn-type freezer, pouring into a mould before it sets completely and freezing for a few more hours until thoroughly frozen. This ice cream freezes quite smoothly without being churned, because of the addition of whipped cream.

'Mamma was asking my father . . . whether M. Swann had had some more of the coffee and pistachio ice. "I thought it rather so-so," she was saying; "next time we shall have to try another flavour." . . . then my father said: "Well, shall we go up to bed?" "As you wish, dear, though I don't feel in the least like sleeping. I don't know why; it can't be the coffee-ice – it wasn't strong enough to keep me awake like this . . ."'

I, 43, 44–5

Pistachio Ice Cream

	UK	US	
750 ml	1¼ pints	3¼ cups	milk
40 g	1½ oz.	⅓ cup	shelled pistachio nuts
45 g	1½ oz.	3 Tb	ground almonds
	5	5	egg yolks
			big pinch of salt
150 g	5 oz.	⅔ cup	caster/fine sugar
	½ tsp	½ tsp	vanilla essence
	2 drops	2 drops	green food colouring (optional)
300 ml	½ pint	1¼ cups	double/heavy cream

Set the oven to gas mark 4, 350° F., and bake the ground almonds for 3 minutes to dry them out.

Put the milk into the top of the double boiler over simmering water. Grind the pistachio nuts in the blender, reserving about a tablespoon for decoration. When the milk is hot, add the nuts and ground almonds, stir, and bring to the boil. Remove from heat, let cool for 5 minutes, and blend in the liquidizer in two batches. Rub through a sieve with a wooden spoon into the top of the double boiler again. These two procedures of blending and sieving are necessary to ensure that the nuts do not make the ice cream grainy. Add half the sugar to the milk.

Proceed as for the coffee ice cream. Beat the yolks and a pinch of salt, using an electric beater if desired, and gradually add the rest of the sugar, beating until the mixture is thick and pale yellow. Pour the hot milk carefully onto the yolks, slowing down the speed of the beater and scraping the side of the bowl with a spatula. Now pour the whole mixture back into the top of the double boiler and stir constantly with a wooden spoon over medium heat until the custard thickens and coats the back of the spoon. Add the vanilla essence and the green food colouring, pour through a sieve into a bowl and let it cool, whisking occasionally to prevent a skin forming on the top. Beat the cream until stiff and fold into the cool custard.

Freeze in an electric ice-cream freezer or a churn-type freezer, pouring into a lightly oiled mould before it sets completely and freezing a few more hours until thoroughly frozen. This ice cream freezes quite smoothly without being churned, because of the addition of whipped cream.

If a bombe mould is available, lightly oil it and coat the inside with coffee ice cream, freezing until stiff and later filling in with pistachio ice cream. Alternatively pour the coffee ice cream into a lightly oiled savarin mould and add the pistachio ice cream later.

Before serving, take the ice cream out of the refrigerator for 15 minutes to soften slightly, cover with a hot damp cloth for a few minutes and unmould onto a platter. Decorate with toasted slivered almonds over the coffee ice cream and additional pistachio nuts over the pistachio ice cream.

Opposite and below : apparatus for making ice cream. *La Cuisine d'aujourd'hui* by Urbain Dubois, 1900.

Blackcurrant Sorbet · Sorbet au Cassis

A water ice, lightened with the addition of beaten egg whites.

		UK	US	
	300 ml	½ pint	1¼ cups	water
	120 g	4 oz.	½ cup	sugar
	450 g	1 lb.	1 lb.	fresh or frozen blackcurrants, cooked for 15 minutes *with*
	150 g	5 oz.	10 Tb	sugar *plus*
		3 Tb	3 Tb	water *or*
		2 tins	2 cans	blackcurrants, 283 g/10 oz. each
				juice of ½ lemon
				juice of 1 orange
	115 ml	4 fl. oz.	½ cup	cassis
		2	2	egg whites

Serves 6

Make a syrup by boiling the water and sugar together for 10 minutes.
Liquidize the blackcurrants and rub through a sieve, discarding the skins.
Add the lemon and orange juice, the cassis and the sugar syrup. Mix together
well and put in a freezer container to freeze overnight, or for at least 8 hours.

Two or three hours before serving, take the ice out of the freezer and
let it soften a little; break up the mass with a fork or better still, using a butter
curler, shave off pieces until it is all soft and grainy. Whip the egg whites until
stiff and fold into the ice mixture with a spatula. Freeze until serving time.

Vanilla Ice Cream · Glace au Vanille

		UK	US	
	750 ml	1¼ pints	3¼ cups	milk
		1	1	vanilla pod (split in two lengthwise)
		5	5	egg yolks
				pinch of salt
	150 g	5 oz.	⅔ cup	caster/fine sugar, sifted
	300 ml	½ pint	1¼ cups	double/heavy cream

Serves 8

It is advisable to flavour the sugar with vanilla beforehand. Measure out the
sugar and put it in a jar with half the vanilla pod for at least a day before
making the ice cream.

Heat the milk with the other half of the vanilla pod in the top of a double
boiler until it is very hot, but not boiling. Remove the pod and stir half the
sugar into the milk. Beat the yolks and a pinch of salt, using an electric beater if
desired, and gradually add the rest of the sugar, beating until the mixture is
thick and pale yellow. Pour the hot milk carefully onto the yolks, slowing
down the speed of the beater and scraping the sides of the bowl with a spatula.
Now pour the mixture back into the top of the double boiler and stir

constantly with a wooden spoon over medium heat until the custard thickens and coats the back of the spoon. Be careful, for this custard can curdle and separate, so avoid over-heating and have patience. When it is thick, pour through a sieve and allow to cool, whisking occasionally to prevent a skin forming on the top.

If the mixture does curdle, quickly pour it through a sieve into a clean saucepan. Beat another egg yolk in a bowl and sieve the mixture in, little by little, constantly beating, to rebuild the emulsion. Refrigerate the mixture.

Beat the cream until stiff, and fold into the cool custard. Freeze in an electric ice-cream freezer or the churn type of freezer, pouring into a lightly oiled mould before it sets completely. Freeze for 2 or more hours or until thoroughly set. This ice cream freezes quite smoothly without being churned, because of the addition of whipped cream.

Remove from refrigerator 15 minutes before serving. To unmould, invert onto a dish and cover with a hot damp teacloth.

Granité au Café

This is a coffee water ice and has, as the name implies, a granular texture.

	UK	US	
120 g	4 oz.	½ cup	sugar
300 ml	½ pint	1¼ cups	water
570 ml	1 pint	2½ cups	strong Continental (after-dinner) coffee
100 ml	1 miniature bottle	6 Tb	coffee liqueur
	1 Tb	1 Tb	toasted almond slivers (see method for toasting, p. 158)
150 ml	¼ pint	⅔ cup	double/heavy cream

Serves 6

Prepare the coffee, being sure to make it very strong. Boil the sugar and water together for 2 minutes. Mix this sugar syrup with the coffee, strain it into an ice tray or shallow container, and leave to cool. When the mixture is cold, add the coffee liqueur and freeze, stirring with a fork occasionally, until a granular mush is formed. There is no need to stir again until just before serving.

Another freezing method (given in the magazine *Marie-Claire*, November 1974) is to pour the cool liquid into a thick bottle, such as a champagne bottle, cork it, and lay it on its side in the freezer. Give the bottle a quarter turn every half an hour until a granular mush is formed. It should not be allowed to freeze to too thick a consistency, partly to avoid any danger of the bottle bursting, and also because it would then be quite difficult to remove from the bottle, although a long skewer or chopstick would be helpful. Giving the bottle quarter turns resembles the *remuage* in the making of champagne.

When ready to serve, whip the cream until stiff, spoon the granité into tall glasses, top with cream and sprinkle with almond slivers.

'At once my anxiety subsided; it was now no longer (as it had been a moment ago) until tomorrow that I had lost my mother . . . for that forbidden and unfriendly dining-room, where but a moment ago the ice itself – with burned nuts in it – and the fingerbowls seemed to me to be concealing pleasures that were mischievous and of a mortal sadness because Mamma was tasting of them and I was far away, had opened its doors to me and, like a ripe fruit which bursts through its skin, was going to pour out into my intoxicated heart the gushing sweetness of Mamma's attention while she was reading what I had written.'

I, 38

Nesselrode Pudding ·
Pudding à la Nesselrode

	UK	US	
120 g	4 oz.	$\frac{3}{4}$ cup	mixed sultanas and raisins
120 g	4 oz.	$\frac{3}{4}$ cup	mixed orange and lemon peel (candied) and chopped glacé cherries (optional)
230 ml	8 fl. oz.	1 cup	Marsala
150 g	5 oz.	$1\frac{1}{2}$ cups	whole cooked chestnuts, fresh, tinned or canned
500 ml	17 fl. oz.	$2\frac{1}{4}$ cups	milk
570 ml	1 pint	$2\frac{1}{2}$ cups	double/heavy cream
	5	5	egg yolks
150 g	5 oz.	$\frac{2}{3}$ cup	sugar
	$1\frac{1}{2}$ tsp	$1\frac{1}{2}$ tsp	vanilla essence
100 ml	6 Tb	6 Tb	cherry brandy or maraschino
120 g	4 oz.	$\frac{3}{4}$ cup	marrons glacés (optional)

Serves 12

' *"What do I see? A Nesselrode pudding! As well! I declare, I shall need a course at Carlsbad after such a Lucullus-feast as this."* '

III, 52

Soak the sultanas, raisins, mixed peel and glacé cherries in the Marsala for 1 hour. Make a custard by beating the yolks with an electric beater in a bowl and gradually adding the sugar until the mixture is thick and pale yellow. Heat the milk in the top of a double boiler until it is nearly boiling and add some to the yolks, lowering the speed of the beater as you do this. Return this mixture to the top of the double boiler and cook over simmering water, stirring constantly, until the mixture thickens and coats the back of the spoon.

This mixture can curdle and it is advisable to keep the water in the double boiler just barely at the boil; stir continuously and be patient! It can be disastrous even to answer the telephone when making custards. When you have achieved this delicious custard, add the vanilla essence, strain into a bowl and leave to cool, whisking occasionally to prevent a skin forming on the top.

Drain the chestnuts if tinned/canned, put them through the fine mesh of the mouli food mill straight into the custard and mix well.

When the custard is cool, whip the cream until stiff, add the maraschino and fold into the custard. Add the mixed fruits and Marsala and pour the mixture into a lightly oiled savarin, kugelhopf or ring mould, or other mould of your choice, and freeze.

Remove from the refrigerator 15 minutes before serving. Invert the mould onto a dish and cover with a hot damp cloth for a few minutes. Surround with marrons glacés (see recipe, p. 149) if desired.

Confectionery

Barley Sugar · Sucre d'Orge

	UK	US	
250 g	9 oz.	1⅓ cups	hulled/pinhead barley
2 litres	3½ pints	9 cups	water
680 g	1½ lb.	3 cups	sugar
	1 Tb	1 Tb	glucose
			red and blue food colouring if desired

Makes ½ kg/1 lb. hard sweets/candies with long-lasting sucking qualities.

Boil the barley and water together in a covered saucepan for 3 hours over very low heat.

Cook the sugar with 2 tablespoons water and the glucose until it reaches 228° F. on the sugar thermometer. Stir down the sugar crystals that form around the edge of the saucepan with a pastry brush dipped in cold water. This is to prevent the sugar from granulating, although the glucose will help.

Strain the barley through a sieve, rubbing the liquid through with a wooden spoon. This whitish opaque liquid should measure approximately 300 ml/10 fl. oz./1½ cups. Stir this liquid into the sugar syrup and cook again until 310° F. (hard crack) on the sugar thermometer. The syrup will take some time before it reaches this point, but as it nears the 300° F. mark watch carefully, for it will heat to 310° F. in a hurry.

Lightly oil a marble slab or counter and pour the syrup over it. Let it cool just a little. With a knife dipped in water, cut ½-inch strips and twist them. It is advisable to have some extra hands to form the barley sugar into twists, because it rapidly cools, hardens and becomes unmalleable. Alternatively pour a third of the syrup at a time onto the marble. Keep the rest warm by placing over a saucepan of simmering water, while shaping the twists.

If desired, colour the barley sugar red and purple by dividing the syrup into two saucepans before boiling to 310° F., adding drops of red to one and red and blue drops to the other, until the appropriate colour is obtained.

'One day, we had gone with Gilberte to the stall of our own special vendor [on the Champs-Elysées] . . . Gilberte pointed out to me with a laugh two little boys who were like the little artist and the little naturalist in the children's story books. For one of them would not have a red stick of rock because he preferred the purple, while the other, with tears in his eyes, refused a plum which his nurse was buying for him.'

II, 254

Kiosk on the Champs Elysées, 1883. Estampes Carnavalet.

Marrons Glacés

	UK	US	
1 kg	2 lb.	2 lb.	chestnuts – choose the large type
680 g	1½ lb.	3 cups	sugar
570 ml	1 pint	2½ cups	water
120 g	4 oz.	¾ cup	glucose (to prevent sugar from crystallizing)
	2 tsp	2 tsp	vanilla essence

'When New Year's Day came, I first of all paid a round of family visits with Mamma. . . . No sooner had we entered the drawing-room of the distant cousin whose claim to being visited first was that her house was at no distance from ours, than my mother was horrified to see standing there, his present of marrons glacés *or* déguisés *in his hand, the bosom friend of the most sensitive of all my uncles, to whom he would at once go and report that we had not begun our round with him.'*

III, 81–2

The chestnuts are shelled and cooked until nearly tender. They are then gradually preserved by macerating them in a vanilla-flavoured sugar syrup which is drained off, made stronger, and poured back on, morning and night, until the chestnuts are thoroughly permeated with the sugar syrup and in a state of delicious preservation. This takes 4 days. Of course it is impossible at home to attain the perfection of the marrons glacés made by the famous *glacier* Faugier, but this recipe produces very adequate and inexpensive ones.

Slit 250 g/½ lb. chestnuts down one side and drop them into boiling water for 10 minutes. Lift out with a slotted spoon or wire spatula, and, trying to keep the chestnuts whole, peel off both the outer shell and inner skin, as quickly as you can, while they are still hot. Once cold, the skin begins to adhere to the nut, so keep the unpeeled chestnuts in hot water.

Repeat with the rest of the chestnuts, boiling 250 g/½ lb. at a time, peeling them and trying to keep them as whole as possible. The broken pieces will taste just as wonderful as the whole chestnuts, so it is worth while preserving them as well.

When all the chestnuts have been shelled, fill a saucepan half full of water with 60 g/2 oz./¼ cup sugar and bring to the boil. Put the chestnuts in carefully, bring to the boil again, then turn the heat down so that the water just barely simmers. Cook the chestnuts until nearly tender. This takes 10 to 20 minutes, depending on the freshness of the chestnuts, so check occasionally; if overcooked they tend to break up in the boiling water. Drain and place in an earthenware dish or a saucepan.

Make a syrup with 350 g/12 oz./1½ cups of the sugar, all the glucose and the water; stir, bring to the boil, and cook for 10 minutes. Pour this syrup over the chestnuts, cover with a teacloth and leave overnight or all day.

Drain off the syrup into a saucepan and add 60 g/2 oz./¼ cup sugar; stir, bring to the boil and cook for 5 minutes. Pour onto the chestnuts and leave overnight or all day again. Repeat this last procedure 4 more times, every morning and evening, adding 1 teaspoon of vanilla essence the last two times.

Leave the chestnuts in the syrup for another half day, turning occasionally, then drain off the syrup and reserve. Spread the chestnuts out on a dish or rack to dry off. Pick out the small broken pieces, add to the reserved syrup and use as a garnish for desserts such as Nesselrode Pudding or Vanilla Ice Cream.

Pack the chestnuts individually in cellophane or cling film/saran wrap, put into little crinkle-edged paper sweet cases and keep in an airtight box or tin. If kept more than a week or so, the sugar in the chestnuts may start to crystallize; in this case it is better to preserve them in their syrup, draining them before use.

Glacé Fruits · Déguisés (Fruits Glacés)

Déguisés are normally fruits dipped in a warm fondant (see *petits fours* recipe, p. 124) and dusted with icing/confectioners' sugar. An easier alternative is glacé fruits.

	UK	US	
450 g	1 lb.	1 lb.	assorted fruits, such as black and white grapes, strawberries, cherries, pineapple, oranges, satsumas, cumquats
350 g	¾ lb.	1½ cups	caster/fine sugar
	1 Tb	1 Tb	glucose or corn syrup (to prevent sugar from crystallizing)
	3 Tb	3 Tb	water

Separate the grapes from the bunch, leaving on their stems. Leave the stems on the cherries and strawberries. Cut the pineapple into small slices; peel the oranges and satsumas, separating them into segments and removing all pith.

Heat the sugar, glucose and water in a saucepan to 240° F. (hard ball stage) on the sugar thermometer. Let cool for 1 minute, then dip the fruits by the stems or on the end of a skewer into the syrup one by one very briefly, letting the syrup drip into the saucepan before placing on a cake rack to cool. Reheat the syrup if it cools and hardens.

Chocolate Drops · Pastilles de Chocolat

	UK	US	
230 g	8 oz.	8 squares	plain or semi-sweet chocolate – Menier, Bournville, or Baker's
	1 Tb	1 Tb	chocolate strands or vermicelli

'. . . the veteran Maréchal de Guermantes, making my nursery-maid's bosom swell with pride, stopped in the Champs-Elysées to remark: "A fine child, that!" and gave me a chocolate drop from his comfit-box.'

v, 6

Break the chocolate into pieces and place it in a bowl over simmering water to melt. When melted, cool for a minute, then spoon into a pastry bag with a ⅜-in. rosette nozzle. Pipe small rosettes onto a lightly oiled surface, such as a marble top or baking sheet. Sprinkle chocolate strands thickly over half the rosettes, leaving the others undecorated. Let cool and harden before storing.

Soft Drinks

Bavaroise

Bavaroise is a comforting hot tea drink, which used to be served at evening parties. The *Bavaroise* (feminine) syrup should not be confused with *Bavarois* (masculine) *à la Crème* or *Bavarois aux Fruits*, which are creams set with gelatin. This recipe makes 2–3 hot drinks.

	UK	US	
15 g	½ oz.	1 Tb	sugar
	2	2	egg yolks
150 ml	¼ pint	⅔ cup	strong hot tea
150 ml	¼ pint	⅔ cup	hot milk

flavouring:

	UK	US	
	1 Tb	1 Tb	kirsch, rum or Cointreau *or* add to the milk:
60 g	2 oz.	2 squares	plain chocolate *or*
	1 Tb	1 Tb	strong coffee *or*
	1 Tb	1 Tb	orange juice *or*
	½ Tb	½ Tb	lemon juice *or*
			piece of vanilla pod

At lunch at Odette Swann's, the ladies discuss the best pâtisseries, concluding: ' "Rebattet for everything iced and syrups [bavaroise] and sorbets . . ." '

III, 252

Make strong tea and heat the milk to boiling. Beat the egg yolks with an electric beater, add the sugar gradually and continue to beat until thick and pale yellow. Add the hot tea and the milk, beating all the time, until frothy and thick. Add the liqueur and pour into glasses.

If desired omit the liqueur and flavour the milk with the required flavouring.

It is possible to freeze this mixture to a tea ice cream.

Redcurrant Syrup · Sirop de Groseilles

Céleste Albaret tells of Proust wanting to drink this syrup in the last years of his life, though he came to prefer ice-cold beer, which she had to send for from the Brasserie Lipp and the Ritz Hotel.

	UK	US	
1 kg	2 lb.	2 lb.	redcurrants
1 kg	2 lb.	2 lb.	sugar

Makes about ¾ litre/1¼ pints/1½ US pints

Pull the redcurrants from their stalks and place in a bowl. Crush the fruit with a pestle or wooden spoon and leave in a cool place for 24 hours.

Rub through the fine mesh of the mouli food mill into a saucepan. Add the sugar, bring to the boil and skim with a slotted spoon. Boil gently for 10 minutes, strain through cheesecloth, allow to cool, and bottle.

Dilute to taste with water.

'I asked Albertine if she would like
something to drink. "I seem to see
oranges over there and water," she said.
"That will be perfect." I was thus able
to taste with her kisses that refreshing
coolness which had seemed to me to be
better than they, at the Princesse de
Guermantes'. And the orange squeezed
into the water seemed to yield to me, as
I drank, the secret life of its ripening
growth, its beneficent action upon
certain states of that human body which
belongs to so different a kingdom, its
powerlessness to make that body live,
but on the other hand the process of
irrigation by which it was able to
benefit it, a hundred mysteries concealed
by the fruit from my senses, but not
from my intellect.'

VII, 192

'M. de Charlus . . . at once conceived a
violent hatred of Mme de Mortemart
and determined to play all sorts of
tricks upon her, such as ordering fifty
iced coffees to be sent to her house on a
day when she was not giving a
party . . .'

X, 87

Orangeade

	UK	US	
	6	6	oranges
120 g	4 oz.	½ cup	caster/fine sugar
150 ml	¼ pint	⅔ cup	water
570 ml	1 pint	2½ cups	iced water
	1 tsp	1 tsp	orangeflower extract
230 ml	8 fl. oz.	1 cup	juice of stewed cherries or pears (optional)

Peel an orange very finely with a potato peeler. Simmer the peel with the sugar and water (not the iced water) for 20 minutes. Leave this syrup to cool. Squeeze the juice of 6 oranges and strain into a jug. Add the iced water, the cooled strained syrup and the orangeflower extract.

Chill the orangeade further by adding a handful of ice cubes. Add the juice of stewed cherries or pears, if desired. Serve immediately.

The peel that has simmered in the sugar syrup is usually delicious to eat, as it will now be candied peel.

Iced Coffee · Café Glacé

	UK	US	
90 g	3 oz.	6 Tb	finely ground after-dinner coffee
430 ml	¾ pint	2 cups	water
120 g	4 oz.	½ cup	caster/fine sugar
570 ml	1 pint	2½ cups	milk
230 ml	8 fl. oz.	1 cup	double/heavy cream

Serves 6–8

Heat the water to boiling, take off the heat, add the coffee, stir and let steep for 15 minutes. Strain through cheesecloth into a jug and stir in the sugar until it is dissolved.

Whisk in the milk and cream and chill thoroughly in the refrigerator.

Add a few ice cubes before serving if desired.

Strawberry Juice · Fraisette

	UK	US	
230 g	½ lb.	½ lb.	strawberries, fresh or frozen
90 g	3 oz.	6 Tb	caster/fine sugar
150 ml	¼ pint	⅔ cup	water
	1 Tb	1 Tb	lemon juice
	3	3	mint leaves (optional)

Makes ½ litre/1 pint 7 fl. oz./3½ cups

Wash, drain and hull the strawberries. If using frozen strawberries, defrost them in the refrigerator until they are just soft and use right away, before they become mushy and discoloured.

Dissolve the sugar in the water over low heat. Let cool. Rub all but 4 of the strawberries through a sieve with a wooden spoon. Add the sugar syrup, mix well and strain through a sieve again into a pitcher or jug. Add the lemon juice, 400 ml/14 fl. oz./2 cups water, the extra strawberries and mint leaves. Cool in the refrigerator and add a handful of ice cubes before serving.

'Refreshments were set out on a table. Mme Verdurin invited the gentlemen to go and choose whatever drinks they preferred. M. de Charlus went and drank his glass and at once returned to a seat by the card-table from which he did not stir. Mme Verdurin asked him: "Have you tasted my orangeade?" Upon which M. de Charlus, with a gracious smile, in a crystalline tone which he rarely sounded and with endless motions of his lips and body, replied: "No, I preferred its neighbour, it was strawberry-juice, I think, it was delicious." '

VIII, 155

Miscellaneous Essentials

Quatre Epices

Quatre épices is a mixture of pepper and spices, used in pâtés and other dishes. It may be bought already ground, in jars, but it is simple to make one's own. The following is a general guide, which can be changed to suit the individual's taste.

Place on a piece of paper

> **3 tsp ground black pepper**
> **1 tsp nutmeg**
> **1 tsp cinnamon**
> **¼ tsp ground cloves**

To mix the spices, fold the paper in two, then unfold and fold in two the other way. Repeat several times. Store in an empty pepper jar.

Ground allspice (also known as *quatre épices* in French) is very similar and may be used instead.

Puff Pastry · Pâte Feuilletée

		UK	US	
450 g	1 lb.	3¾ cups	flour	
450 g	1 lb.	4 sticks	unsalted butter	
230 ml	8 fl. oz.	1 cup	water (approximate quantity)	
			pinch of salt	

Makes 1 kg/2¼ lb.

Sift the flour together with the salt into a large bowl. Make a well in the flour and add most of the water and ½ oz. of the butter. Mix together gradually with a fork until a rough dough is obtained, adding more water if necessary. Turn out onto a board or counter and knead, using extra flour if needed, for 10 minutes or until the dough becomes smooth and elastic. Wrap in a teacloth and let rest for 20 minutes.

Roll out the dough on a floured board or counter to a large square approximately 16 inches square.

Soften the butter with your hands under cold water or work it with a knife until soft and pliable. It should have the same consistency as the dough.

Now place the butter in the centre of the dough and pull the corners of the dough over the butter so that it is completely covered. Roll out a rectangle approximately 21 in. long by 7 in. wide, the length of the rectangle stretching away from you. Fold the rectangle of dough into three. Turn the dough so that the side edges are facing you. Close the edges with a little pressure from the rolling pin, to prevent the butter from squeezing out. Roll out to a long rectangle again. Fold into three again, turn and close edges again. You have now rolled and 'turned' twice. Wrap in a cloth or plastic bag and put it to 'rest' in the refrigerator for 20 minutes. Take out and repeat rolling and 'turning' four more times, adding more flour, if needed, to the board or counter and putting to 'rest' after each 2 turns, or more often if the butter starts to break through the dough.

Mark the number of times you turn the dough by making little indentations on it with the fingertips. It should have six turns in all (seven in summer). It can be used right away or, if need be, stored for up to two days in the refrigerator, or frozen.

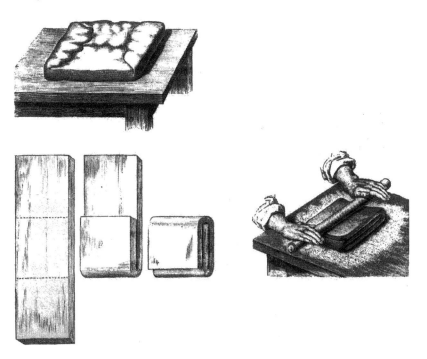

The making of puff pastry. *La Cuisine d'aujourd'hui* by Urbain Dubois, 1900.

Puff Pastry Crescents · Fleurons

These pastry crescents are useful to garnish certain dishes, such as Fillets of Sole au Vin Blanc, Creamed Spinach, Brill with Cream Sauce. Use puff pastry trimmings if available or:

	US	US	
100 g	3½ oz.	3½ oz.	puff pastry (see above) *or* frozen puff pastry – defrosted
	1	1	egg yolk
	1 tsp	1 tsp	milk

Roll out pastry to a thickness of ⅛ in. Using a fluted-edged pastry cutter 3 in. in diameter, cut out a series of crescents.

Set the oven to gas mark 6, 400° F. Brush a baking sheet with water, place the crescents on the sheet, and brush with the egg yolk beaten with the milk.

Bake for 15 minutes, when they should be puffed and golden.

Rice · Riz

	UK	US	
		1 scant	
200 g	7 oz.	cup	long grain rice
200 ml	7 fl. oz.	1 cup	water
	1 tsp	1 tsp	salt
15 g	½ oz.	1 Tb	butter

Serves 3–4

Rinse the rice thoroughly.

Put all the ingredients into a saucepan, cover, and bring to the boil over high heat. As soon as the rice comes to the boil, turn the heat to very, very low, so that it barely simmers. Leave to cook without stirring for 25–30 minutes, depending on how low the heat has been. More cold water may be added if necessary during the cooking. The lower the heat, the slower the evaporation of the liquid.

The water is completely absorbed and the rice needs only to be lightly forked into a serving dish. It will remain warm and fluffy for a further half hour if kept in the same covered saucepan until serving time.

Pralin

For use in cake making or to sprinkle over ice cream.

	UK	US	
180 g	6 oz.	1 cup	almonds or hazelnuts
180 g	6 oz.	¾ cup	vanilla sugar
75 ml	3 fl. oz.	6 Tb	water

To roast almonds:

Buy best Jordan almonds and drop them into boiling water for 5 minutes. Drain off the water and when cool enough to handle slip off the skins. Set the oven to gas mark 4, 350° F. Lay the nuts on a baking sheet and bake for 20 minutes until they are a pale brown.

To roast hazelnuts:

Set the oven to gas mark 5, 375° F. Place the nuts on a baking sheet and bake for 10 minutes until the skins are brown. Wrap the nuts in a teacloth and rub to remove the skins.

Boil the water and sugar together over medium heat until the syrup turns a pale caramel colour. Off the heat, stir in the roasted nuts and pour out onto a lightly oiled marble top or counter. When cool, break into pieces and pulverize in a blender, meat grinder, or mortar and pestle. Keep in an airtight box.

Custard Cream · Crème Anglaise

This custard cream, when cold, is a perfect base for fruit tarts, such as strawberry tarts (see recipe, p. 129), or delicious served with a fruit salad. It can be used in the Normandy puff pastries (see recipe, p. 127) and served warm with hot desserts, such as stewed fruits. It can be flavoured with kirsch, rum or orange or lemon rind.

	UK	US	
	4	4	egg yolks
60 g	2 oz.	¼ cup	caster/fine sugar
300 ml	½ pint	1¼ cups	milk
			pinch of salt
	¼	¼	vanilla pod, split

Heat the milk until warm in the top of a double boiler.

Beat the egg yolks in a bowl, using an electric beater if desired. Gradually add the sugar and beat until the mixture is thick and pale yellow. Lower the speed of the beater, pour in the warm milk and add the salt. Pour back into the top of the double boiler, scraping the bowl well. Add the split vanilla pod and stir constantly with a wooden spoon over barely simmering water, until the mixture thickens and coats the back of the spoon. Overheating can cause the mixture to curdle, so do have patience.

Pour the cream through a sieve into a bowl and whisk occasionally until cool. Then cover the surface with greaseproof paper (to prevent a skin from forming) and chill in the refrigerator.

Vanilla Sugar · Sucre Vanillé

Vanilla sugar is an ingredient essential to many cakes, biscuits and desserts.

It is simple to have always on hand a glass jar with a close-fitting lid, filled with about 450 g/1 lb. caster/fine sugar with a vanilla pod inserted in it. The aroma and flavour of the vanilla pod permeates the sugar, and its use eliminates the need for vanilla essence.

Remember to replace the sugar as you use it and to renew the vanilla pod every six months or so.

Illustration by Madeleine Lemaire from Proust's *Les Plaisirs et les jours*, 1896.

INDEX